TWELVE CASES

A PSYCHIATRIST'S TRUE STORIES OF MENTAL ILLNESS AND ADDICTION

[and other human predispositions]

DANIEL MIERLAK, MD, PHD

LUMINARE PRESS
WWW.LUMINAREPRESS.COM

AUTHOR'S NOTE

The following cases are true, but to protect the individuals involved, names, dates, locations, and other identifying details have been scrupulously changed. It is important to note that no claim is made as to how psychiatric disorders ought to be treated, and none should be taken from the specific treatments mentioned.

Earlier versions of
What is the Heroin? and *The Worst Call in the World* previously published on Huffington Post.

TWELVE CASES
A Psychiatrist's True Stories of Mental Illness and Addiction and Other Human Predispositions

©2018 Daniel Mierlak, MD, PhD

All rights reserved. This book or any portion thereof may not be reproduced or used in any manner whatsoever without the express written permission of the publisher, except for the use of brief quotations in a book review.

Printed in the United States of America

Cover Design by Claire Flint Last

Luminare Press
438 Charnelton St., Suite 101
Eugene, OR 97401
www.luminarepress.com

LCCN: 2018947198
ISBN: 978-1-944733-81-0

For Bronwyn, Deryn, and Donovan

Everything has been figured out,
except how to live.

—JEAN-PAUL SARTRE

TABLE OF CONTENTS

Preface 1

CASE ONE
First, Do No Harm 7

CASE TWO
The Letter 39

CASE THREE
The Manilow Paradox 53

CASE FOUR
The Worst Call In
The World 67

CASE FIVE
My Time is Gonna Come 83

CASE SIX
Glass of Water 109

CASE SEVEN
The Bosnian Surgeon 119

CASE EIGHT
What is the Heroin? 133

CASE NINE
Revelations 143

CASE TEN
Making Movies 157

CASE ELEVEN
The Illusion of Depth 173

CASE TWELVE
The Longer You Stay 191

Afterword 201

Acknowledgments 203

PREFACE

JUDGING FROM THE QUESTIONS I'VE gotten over the years when someone new learns I'm a psychiatrist, many people seem genuinely curious about what goes on inside the office of a shrink. And why shouldn't they be curious? The capacity of human beings to surprise, and to shock, is impressive. The media is full of reports. Perhaps you've noticed stories recently of unseemly behavior from public figures? Or how about these examples much closer to home—reflect on *your own* fantasy life for a few minutes, or, better yet, behaviors that you keep secret, or wish you could. If you're honest you'll have to agree with me—we are *all* capable of the provocative.

There's no question that psychiatrists do some of their work with patients out on the darker edges of the psyche. Who wouldn't be interested to hear about that exotic landscape? The stranger versions of human experience are just plain fascinating to so many of us. And even if you claim disinterest in matters of psychopathology, even if the lurid is not your particular cup of tea, at the very least it can reassure to learn that some people out there have more issues than you do. I completely understand these brands of curiosity—after all, I decided to pursue psychiatry as a specialty nearly thirty years ago.

But psychiatry is not like other medical disciplines. The sensitive nature of the symptoms we delve—involving as they do our thoughts, emotions, and behaviors—sets a higher bar for confidentiality. Because of this, access to authentic accounts of psychiatric practice, for the general audience, is harder to come by. Yet, flying in the face of this thoughtful discretion, there seems to be no shortage of *popular culture stereotypes* of psychiatrists and psychiatric patients—in films, television, and fiction writing. Like all caricatures, these depictions lack nuance and are easy prey for the cynical to belittle a couple of already beleaguered groups.

You would think that so long as I kept identity secret I'd be in a good position to satisfy the inquiring mind about the private conversations I have with patients, and set the record straight on biased misconceptions. Despite a career of it though, I must admit, it has not been easy to explain my work. I've had trouble when asked to describe what *the practice of* psychiatry is really like. My responses have been too often generic and fail to hit the mark, as this exchange with my kids, one of many attempted, demonstrates vividly:

"I help people with their problems by talking to them, and sometimes giving them medicine."

"What kinda problems, Dad?...What do the medicines do?...You talk to 'em and they get better?...You get *paid* for just *talking* to people!?..."

OK, so maybe the profession is, legitimately, somewhat opaque.

On the other hand I may be taking the wrong approach to try to summarize psychiatry—it seems an inherently lame exercise. As I've thought about it, there is probably a simple reason blanket statements about psychiatry don't work. It's the same reason blanket statements about romantic comedies don't work. People are interested in *stories* with *characters* and *action*, not formulas. And in psychiatry, as I've come to see, it's the *story of the treatment*—the meandering journey of collaboration between patient and doctor—that lies at the very center of the curiosity which yearns to be a fly on the shrink's wall.

Therefore, I present the following twelve cases as my answer to what it's like to be a psychiatrist. Think of each as a stroll through a single gallery of a very large museum. In these stories I take you away from fictional, stigmatized renditions of psychiatry and instead drop you into actual hospital wards, into my private office, and in one instance, into a house call. The way psychosis, mania, and depression unfold—the particulars of four-point restraint, electroconvulsive therapy, and overnight call—the management of suicidality and homicidality—and the wild horse of addictive disorders—are some of the circumstances that await you.

Strange as these real accounts read, the underlying struggles they reveal are familiar. At heart these are stories of individuals who grapple with their demons—

something that I suspect can resonate with us all—remember my little thought experiment about your own fantasies and behaviors? You will find a part of yourself somewhere in these tales.

On a personal note, I sometimes get asked how the work with psychiatric patients has affected me. I trust some of the unusual challenges I have faced will come through in the cases described in this volume. You can decide for yourself how well I negotiated them. The truth is, the unexpected plays such a central role in psychiatric practice that it's impossible to succinctly sum up the impact of a career in psychiatry on oneself. But I'll try anyway.

If there's one thing I've learned from working with patients it's this: as much as we think we know someone, ourselves included, there's always more.

So now, for those interested in a rare glimpse, if I may open the door, please follow me inside…

CASE ONE

FIRST, DO NO HARM

A popular storyteller's device is to start at the beginning, and to the extent this collection traverses an arc, it fits that our first case is almost literally the first case of my career as psychiatrist. It occurred during the initial weeks of residency training and takes us deep into the psychiatric hospital.

Anyone who remembers the anxiety of starting a new job, or a new school, or a new anything, will realize some familiarity in this account. As for the rest of the details I hope few find recognition, for the action described concerns paranoia and violence. That this case unfolds on a locked inpatient psychiatric unit is apt—certain impulses are best managed in protected spaces.

The therapeutic relationship between doctor and patient is where the work of psychiatry takes place.

It is prudent for the psychiatrist to remember that patients can form profound attachments within that space.

IT ALL STARTED WITH A SLAP IN THE FACE.

July 1990. I was a freshly minted MD, less than two weeks into internship, the first year of residency training for all physicians. Psychiatry had a four-year residency, and the internship year consisted of rotations on the hospital services for medicine, neurology, and psychiatry. I had drawn a schedule that started with six weeks of inpatient psychiatry. Tactically speaking, this was bad luck. In a year that would crush my notion of endurance with brutal stretches of overnight call and endless tasks on very sick patients, the psychiatry rotation was considered vacation time. Case in point: there was no overnight duty for interns on psychiatry. Not only did I lose the option to have a soft rotation later in the year, even worse, I would start medicine six weeks behind all my colleagues. They would be weathered, and I wouldn't have developed any calluses yet.

The psychiatric hospital I trained at was the Payne Whitney Clinic, part of the renowned New York Hospital-Cornell Medical Center in Manhattan. The Clinic stood separate from the main hospital complex and was connected by an underground tunnel. There were five units for inpatient psychiatry, each on a different floor. The second-year psychiatry residents ran three of the units. The remaining two were smaller, one run by faculty (the attending unit), and the last a research unit focused on schizophrenia. Interns were assigned to the attending unit for their psychiatry rotation.

Even though it took admissions from the same patient pool as the resident-run units, the attending unit was known to be temperamentally calmer. This cut both ways for the intern. On the one hand it meant a gentler introduction to the most difficult psychiatric patients, but on the other hand it could feel like a coddled, watered down version of what was to come in the second year.

I arrived on the attending unit, Payne Whitney 5, one early July morning to learn I was getting an admission. Still a rookie to the whole process of admitting patients, my pulse quickened. The patient was a transfer from the fourth floor—Payne Whitney 4, one of the resident units—and had been admitted there from the emergency room just hours earlier. This was very unusual. Patients were rarely transferred between units. There was a tense vibe among the nursing staff; they had already been briefed on the case. The patient had been admitted to Payne Whitney 4 once previously, about a year ago. The nurses had good reason to be nervous. This patient, a woman, had just assailed the fourth-floor head nurse.

Upon arrival to work that same morning, the Payne Whitney 4 day-shift must have felt disoriented. Their newest patient had already commandeered the energy and attention of the entire unit. Dressed in a hospital gown, she ran up and down the long hallway agitated, shouting threats. When she came upon the head nurse she was stopped by a startled recognition. Within the patient's disordered mental processes was the conviction that the head nurse had assaulted her during last year's admission. After screaming this delusional accusation to the gathered staff yielded little satisfaction, the patient roundly slapped the head nurse across her face.

One of the most important functions of the psychiatric hospital is to offer safe and humane treatment for patients whose illnesses inspire violent impulses. The necessity for patient and society is obvious. Equally obvious is the likelihood that these patients, until effectively treated, will discharge their aggression within the walls of the hospital. Staff are trained to manage such events but each is unique, and often escalates rapidly, and always evokes the fight or flight response, from every witness.

The protocol after an assault is standard and was well known to the experienced staff of the fourth floor.

The patient is approached by a group of five or six staff members. There is one spokesperson, agreed upon beforehand. With this show of force evident, the spokesperson calmly, and with a firm but neutral voice, tells the patient that they need to regain control of their behavior. They are usually instructed to go to a quiet area for a period of time to recover their composure. Sometimes medicine is administered.

In this case the patient was escorted to the seclusion room—a featureless room, empty except for a mattress on the floor, and whose sturdy door housed a small, single pane of thick Plexiglas. Despite her agreement to a tranquilizer, she did not quiet. On the contrary she remained quite agitated—screaming and banging on the locked door. When she recognized another staff member from last year's admission her verbal threats escalated and began to target him. At that point it was clear she couldn't be treated on the fourth floor and the transfer was decided. I think breakfast hadn't even concluded yet.

The patient was escorted the one floor up to my unit by a phalanx of large male staff members. She was immediately placed in the private room closest to the nurse's station. In addition to all this special attention, her hospital gown further set her apart from the other patients. They wore clothes brought from home.

I decided to give her some time to settle down, have some food, maybe take a shower. I also wanted to review her chart and learn more before introducing myself, so

I took her thick binder to a quiet corner of the nurse's station and started to read.

Her name was Amanda K. She was raised in Oregon, one of six children. Her parents divorced when she was eight; she then lived with various relatives. She described herself as always impulsive and moody. After high school she moved to Los Angeles and started working.

Two years ago she moved to New York and her fortunes began to change. The moodiness and impulsivity amplified. She had a series of secretarial jobs that ended with her abrupt dismissal, or her abrupt decision to quit, usually after an angry outburst. She met her current boyfriend about a year and a half ago and moved in with him. This relationship did not have a stabilizing influence. She started to have bouts of paranoia during which she believed others acted malevolently against her. Emboldened by an impulse control in retreat, her retaliatory nature caused her to respond to these perceived perpetrators as you would expect: she began to punch and kick strangers on the street because of "what they had done" to her. The boyfriend was not immune. Their increasingly volatile relationship achieved crisis status last year when she splashed Pine Sol into his eyes during a dust up. That landed him in the ER, and her on Payne Whitney 4 the first time. In two years she had gone from difficult to disturbed.

It was during that first admission at Payne Whitney that her diagnosis was narrowed down to a severe personality disorder vs. bipolar disorder (manic-depressive illness). Both conditions can produce elements of the clinical picture she presented with. But because other symptoms were teased out of the history (spending sprees, hypersexuality, periods of decreased sleep and increased energy), the bipolar diagnosis was favored and she began a trial of Lithium, the gold standard treatment for bipolar disorder. Unfortunately for all, she didn't respond. Her hospital stay was filled with suspiciousness, hostility, visits to the seclusion room, and numerous rounds of medication to try and calm her internal storm.

With only marginal improvement to show, she was nonetheless discharged from Payne Whitney 4 after a couple of weeks and referred to our outpatient psychiatry clinic for follow-up. For six months she cycled through a series of powerful mood stabilizer medications for bipolar disorder. Each medicine produced an intolerable side effect and little benefit for the core symptoms. Our inability to help her was exemplified by the manner in which the treatment ended. The patient abruptly terminated after accusing her (female) therapist of sexual advances.

After that, for a few months, she was not engaged in any treatment, not taking any medication, and not getting any better. On two separate occasions she ran into staff from the fourth floor in the vicinity of the hospital. She assaulted them both, and railed to the onlookers about her mistreatment. These were the same staff targeted by the patient this morning.

About two months ago her fortunes changed again. She became depressed. The aggression and paranoia quieted. She became withdrawn, then suicidal. In this melancholic state she brought herself to the St. Vincent's emergency room in lower Manhattan. They admitted her but made a critical mistake: they did not take a careful history. Limiting their inquiry to present symptoms only, St. Vincent's formulated her diagnosis as atypical depression. They missed the bipolar disorder.

The atypical depression conjecture led them to Parnate, one of the most powerful antidepressants available. Problem is, in a bipolar patient, Parnate can act as jet fuel and propel the mood out of depression, then through the entirety of the normal mood range, and into full mania. They unwittingly gave the patient a medication that would very likely return her to the paranoid-driven aggression she had no control of, and no insight into.

It didn't happen right away. Initially, the medication lifted her out of depression and into a reasonably neutral mood. The suicidal urges dispelled, and the patient was indebted to be out of that hole. She saw Parnate as her savior from the darkness. Although feisty during that admission at St. Vincent's, she required no seclusion and was discharged before any shenanigans occurred.

Six weeks later, she was back at the St. Vincent's ER. The Parnate had done its work. She was agitated, angry, fighting with strangers, and unable to sleep. The hospital realized their error, admitted her again, and quickly added Lithium for the bipolar process. They knew they had to slam the brakes on Parnate since it had become an accelerant to her mania. They began to lower the dose and explained the rationale to the patient. It didn't go well. The patient became enraged that Parnate, the only medicine that had ever helped her, was being removed. After that she refused to take any medication whatsoever, stopped participating in treatment, and demanded to be discharged. Apparently St. Vincent's had had enough of her, so they obliged and let her go. That was three days ago. Now, she was in the room next door to me, paranoid, hostile, and fresh from an assault on a staff member. I closed the chart, placed it back in the rack, and took a deep breath.

Reading the chart did not allay my anxiety. Actually, it had the opposite effect. I was a greenhorn to inpatient psychiatry and the dark capacities of the human mind. The most difficult patient I had managed thus far was Mr. Feldman, a schizophrenic rabbinical student who believed Jesus was a tall, blonde man with a large phallus. Peanuts. Amanda was the real deal, hatched from the reptilian brain, and she stirred up some old fears in me.

I may have been new to psychiatry but I was not a stranger to fear—I had my own secrets like everyone else. Since a little boy, I'd been deeply, paralytically, phobic of hospitals—a result of my first visit to one on a Sunday to see my ailing grandfather, who unluckily died the next day. Briefly unattended in that astringent hospital room, I pulled back the curtain and saw my shriveled grandfather in a heap on the bed, vacant eyes wide open, gasping for breath. The ghastly image, seared into my mind's eye, was re-experienced every Sunday night for years to come and turned bedtime into a losing battle against memory.

Going to medical school was, among other motives, my counter-phobic reaction to the terror of hospitals—sort of like becoming a professional cliff diver to get over a fear of heights. The thought of meeting Amanda tickled me in that sensitive spot for some reason. I became afraid again. But now, as I had done many times as a medical student, I beat down the fear and turned to the task in front of me. Right now, it was time to introduce myself and attempt to interview Amanda K.

I knocked and entered her room, accompanied by a nurse who had tranquilizer medication at the ready. Several male staff members remained outside and watched us through the Plexiglas.

Amanda looked like she had been through hell. Seated on the bed and dressed in a hospital gown worked over with sweat, hair greasy and unkempt, she appeared simultaneously exhausted and wired. The room felt full of static electricity, an invisible energy ready to combust. To complete the strange scene, her arms shook with an uncontrollable coarse tremor. Whether caused by the medications she had received or her condition itself, the rhythmic flapping had a metronomic precision, and closed the case that Amanda's brain wasn't in proper working order at all.

"Good Morning Ms. K., I'm Dr. Mierlak. I'll be working with you here on the fifth floor. How are you feeling?"

Amanda tried to cooperate but her wheels were spinning too fast. With a breathless desperation she launched into a series of pressured tangents—disconnected thoughts that conveyed great sadness, helplessness, and outrage. Her outward manner shifted uncannily from tears to threats, which induced a sense of vertigo in the room. It was like walking into the middle of an absurdist one-woman monologue that sped up by the minute. She was insistent the staff of the fourth floor had hurt her in the past. As Amanda accelerated, her anger started to feed upon itself. Ignition seemed imminent.

I interrupted her, "Talking about this is very upsetting for you. Let us give you some medication to calm things down." Not missing a beat, the nurse stepped forward and offered the tranquilizer pill. Which Amanda resolutely slapped out of her hand and across the room.

What happened next I had never seen before.

The staff stationed outside had witnessed Amanda's action and immediately entered the room. Amanda, super-fueled by adrenaline and paranoia, saw her fears realized as the squadron of staff approached her *and threw herself into their midst*, flailing with an animal-like ferocity. The men physically subdued her and placed her face down on the bed. Out of nowhere a hypodermic appeared. Amanda received her medication after all, injected deeply into the muscle of her buttock as she clawed, spat, and howled at the injustice. It probably took thirty seconds in total. Rendered immobile as reaction to Amanda's loss of control, and the staff's macabre choreography that sought to reinstate it, I quickly came out of my spell and remembered to breathe—no small feat given that my heartbeat pounded against my eardrums.

The staff assembled in the nurse's station after this event to have "the post"—a review of the incident. Part quality control, part support group, the exercise occurred after every important incident on the unit. The staff knew I had never been through such a disturbing event; it was so early in the academic year. After a review of their actions—what went well, what didn't, whether it could have been avoided—they made sure to ask me how I was doing. That was kind, but I really wasn't sure at all how I was doing.

Interns and residents received supervision on their casework from an assigned faculty member. These supervisory sessions were scheduled, like everything else, into the activities of the workweek. This case was not suited to scheduled appointments however. I sought out my supervisor for an impromptu talk and we tried to make sense of what was going on, and what had just happened. It was a highly speculative discussion. After that I returned to my other patients on the unit, all of who seemed in excellent mental health by comparison, even Mr. Feldman. I did not see Amanda again that day; she was on autopilot with nursing. Just as well. I had stirred enough waters for one day.

Amanda K.'s evening went poorly. She became agitated and threatening whenever staff entered her room with food or medication. Something went very wrong during the overnight because when I came in the next morning, Amanda was in four-point restraint.

Four-point restraint is, just as it sounds, complete immobilization. The patient is placed on a bed or gurney, on their back with arms at the sides. Padded leather straps are fastened to the bed frame and then wrists and ankles are secured within the straps. It is impossible to get out of restraint by oneself, but one can struggle against them and work up a good sweat.

Restraint is reserved for the most serious behavioral loss of control. It is an emergency procedure not initiated lightly; the patient has often committed a violent act against themselves or others on the unit, and isn't de-escalating. They are not responding to redirection by staff, or to medication, or they are not allowing medication to be administered. It's not a nuanced predicament. These patients are grossly out of control, and the intervention to restrain is designed to keep them and those around them safe from harm. There are strict protocols for these situations. For example, each restraint must be released every fifteen minutes so that the limb can be flexed and its range of motion assessed.

Most patients regain control of their behavior relatively quickly after being placed in restraint. The immobilization prevents further harm and safely buys time for medication to kick in and calm down. Amanda did not fall into this category. Despite two intramuscular injections of tranquilizer, she spent most of the night in a struggle against the restraints, as vile curses, spittle, and paranoid rants spewed unabated. The meds weren't touching her. Was Amanda some kind of elite neurochemical athlete?

Then suddenly, like a fever breaks, she became calm. At the 11 a.m. limb range of motion assessment she was cooperative. The nurses spoke with her and were reassured; they removed the restraints. Amanda took a shower and lunch was brought into her room. It seemed the crisis was settling down.

I knocked at her door, entered, and attempted my second interview. Amanda was again seated on the bed in her hospital gown, half-eaten lunch nearby. The shower had made a big difference. Given the past twenty-four hours she was eerily subdued. With an unexpectedly pleasant conversational style, we discussed her newfound control. I thought, *"OK, the meds have kicked in. We can work with this."*

Then she dropped the grenade. "Where's my Parnate?" Of course I remembered what happened at St. Vincent's four days earlier when Amanda asked them the same question. It would test my powers of persuasion but ethically I had to tell her. What choice did I have? She seemed reasonable now, I told myself, and hopefully would understand why the medication had to be discontinued.

I picked up the grenade and started to lay out the case. The Parnate was fuel for the rage that led her back to the St. Vincent's ER, and then to us, I explained. It had to be stopped to give her a chance to regain control. As I spoke I saw Amanda's lucidity evaporate before my eyes. First the face, then the body, stiffened and coiled. Leap-frogging across the entire spectrum of reason, she began to frantically beg me not to stop the Parnate. I would be taking away her life, she pleaded. I don't think I said anything but it didn't matter. She was in a psychotic free fall, her fears cascading into the abyss of delusional rage. In less than a minute she became convinced I was an assassin. Terrified, she began to throw objects at me—the bed linens, pillows, lunch tray. She ripped a lamp from its socket and hurled it. I ducked, and then fled the room.

A small battalion of staff quickly gathered for the intervention to place Amanda back in restraints. At least I would be prepared for this one. As the staff assembled I peered through the Plexiglas panel in Amanda's door. The room was trashed. She stood defiant, ready for an attack, brandishing an electric fan that was still plugged into the wall. I looked down at her feet. She was barefoot, and stood in a puddle of orange juice.

The staff rushed her, disarmed her, and forcibly placed her back in four-point restraint. It was rapid and violent. My reaction was muted. Had I already become desensitized?

This case had gotten out of control, our control. Within the first twenty-four hours on our unit, Amanda had assaulted numerous staff, been in restraints twice, received several emergency intramuscular injections, and nearly electrocuted herself. I may have been a rookie but I knew we weren't close to gaining the upper hand on her mania, and I could see the clenched muscles in the faces of the staff.

We called in Dr. A., Payne Whitney's expert on violence in psychiatric patients. He reviewed the case and declared Amanda "an emergency." Although I didn't know exactly where his authority came from, Dr. A.'s imprimatur allowed us to now administer any medication we wished, whether Amanda agreed or not. Attention shifted to Amanda's psychosis, the delusional beliefs that others had harmed her. Perhaps if her psychosis were targeted specifically we could break the back of the agitation and violence.

We decided to try Haldol, a powerful antipsychotic medication with established, robust action against psychotic symptoms. Haldol was a heavy hitter, it could bring down the fiercest psychosis, but it also carried the risk of some nasty side effects. A twice a day dosing schedule was determined. Because of her emergency status, Amanda would get the dose as an intramuscular shot if she refused the pill. The tranquilizers, medicines more specific for anxiety, had done little so far but would remain available for agitation as needed. With this plan in place we began to dose the Haldol and waited for it to quell the psychosis. It was Friday night when the new protocol started.

I had a welcomed weekend off. My vestigial fear of the hospital, reactivated briefly by Amanda, retreated back into its deep, psychic sack. Swapped in its place, I noticed that being so close to unbridled aggression and violence drained the energy out of me, and after a long sleep I awoke wondering if I could handle a career of this.

When I came back to Payne Whitney 5 on Monday I learned that Amanda had spent the whole weekend in restraints, agitated and abusive, once striking a staff member during the range of motion assessment. She received six intramuscular injections. I interviewed her while she lay restrained. Amanda's clinical picture had changed. She was now less coherent, expressed new delusions, and appeared to have visual hallucinations. Unbelievably, she was worse.

Amanda's room looked like the medicine service—IV poles, blood pressure cuffs, bed pans, urinals, blood drawing paraphernalia, etc. There were two nurses present at all times. She was getting blood drawn every day and there was evidence of muscle breakdown, probably a combination of her struggle against the restraints and the intramuscular injections. We decided to back off on the shots.

While the unit was shifting to a medicine/psychiatry mind set, I was approached by nursing with a new problem. A man who claimed to be Amanda's husband had been calling the nurse's station for days, for permission to visit his wife. He had been denied entry to the unit for obvious reasons. Frustrated, and on the phone right now, he insisted on a meeting with his wife's doctor. "Of course I'll speak with you," I responded, and suggested we meet in the hospital's lobby.

Mr. K. came over in short order. I found him in the lobby, pacing, and motioned to a pair of chairs in a quiet corner. After humorless introductions I asked how long they had been married, and it came out that he and Amanda were not actually married, a detail Mr. K. waved off as irrelevant. Naturally he was very concerned about Amanda's welfare and wanted to see her, and was confused and alarmed about why his access to the unit had been stonewalled.

I apologized to Mr. K. for our neglect to keep him in the loop on Amanda's condition, and reassured him that she was well cared for. However, Amanda was very sick, and we felt it would upset him greatly, and probably her, to visit. Mr. K. remarked that he'd seen Amanda ill before, so that wasn't an issue. And anyway, didn't he have a right to see his wife? Well, she really was *quite* ill, and there was still the concern that seeing him could agitate *her* further. K. wasn't buying it, and kept up his insistence that it was his right to see her. My instinct told me not to correct Mr. K. and point out he *wasn't actually* Amanda's husband. No matter what other angle I played, K. repeated his demand to see Amanda, each iteration stoking more frustration in him. Finally, I said, "I'm sorry, but you have to trust our judgment. I'll call you as soon as Amanda is well enough for a visit."

K. stopped speaking and looked me square in the eyes. We sat together silent and stared at each other, unblinking, a game of chicken. Until he spoke.

"Doctor. I fought in the Iran-Iraq war."

He paused. I said nothing.

"I've killed soldiers." Another pause.

"yes…?" I feebly managed.

"I just want you to know. I have killed men before."

Needless to say, I was *not* prepared for *this*. *Did he just make a death threat?* Adrenaline poured into my bloodstream, activating a primeval pathway in my brain. I needed to get the hell away from K., ASAP. I stood, and despite the mayhem in my chest, managed to push air through a larynx in constriction. "You'll be contacted when Amanda can have visitors," I croaked, and then dispatched myself with haste to the elevator.

Wobbling, I went straight to my supervisor and related the lobby discussion. "Maybe you should enter and leave the hospital through the loading dock for a while." Sound advice. I would start that immediately, and also scan everyone on the street, and also look back over my shoulder frequently. I was now uneasy both inside *and* outside the hospital. This case had perforated the doctor-patient boundary, and had become way too personal.

Meanwhile, we watched Amanda's condition closely. She continued to deteriorate. The day after the injections stopped she became delirious: disoriented to time and place, hallucinating, arms and legs rigid. Her sensitive brain, compromised by the manic episode to begin with, was now in gross malfunction. Delirium can be life-threatening if the cause is not identified and corrected. The medical work-up intensified. Multiple consults were called and a flurry of tests performed to determine the cause of her delirium. In the end the consensus was that Amanda had a rare drug reaction—neuroleptic malignant syndrome, or NMS. Antipsychotics, like the Haldol she had been given, are neuroleptics. In NMS, for unclear reasons, these drugs, especially if given by intramuscular injection, initiate a toxic cascade of brain dysfunction. Amanda met most of the criteria for NMS. The treatment was to stop the neuroleptic, which we had already done, support her vital signs, and wait for the syndrome to run its course.

In hindsight, we had triggered a most unfortunate unintended consequence via the neuroleptic Haldol. To be fair there were limited choices. Amanda was acutely ill and dangerously out of control, and demanded emergency intervention. After the tranquilizers didn't work there was no other class of drug that made sense. The NMS was a stroke of bad luck to say the least, particularly for Amanda.

Over the next three days the staff of Payne Whitney 5 vigorously supported Amanda's bodily functions. In spite of nursing care that would have made the medical service proud, the syndrome gathered steam. On the fourth day she spiked a fever and a bunch of her labs bumped up to dangerous levels. Amanda could no longer be cared for safely on a psychiatric unit, and so she was transferred to the medical ICU at New York Hospital. Amidst the sense of relief that we could now exhale, a unit-wide emotional exhaustion followed her transfer. There aren't many cases where this much goes wrong. Thank God.

Officially off the case I followed Amanda's progress nonetheless. The NMS crested and broke rather quickly in the ICU. The aftermath of the delirium ironically left her somewhat improved with regard to the mania. After a full medical recovery Amanda was transferred to another psychiatric hospital to finish treatment. No one contacted me after that.

During my time at Payne Whitney I would witness the range of human travails that came to the psychiatric hospital's door. It was humbling, here at the outset of my training, to see so graphically what could be unleashed when one lost complete control of one's *self*, the being that negotiates with aggressive impulses, that evaluates suspicion by the benchmark of reality. It humbled just as much to see the limits of the ministrations available to these most afflicted patients. The staff seemed to have found an acceptance of these truths. They never judged or blamed Amanda; they simply provided the care required at each moment. The case had encompassed only nine days but, for better or worse, I was no longer a rookie—I felt seasoned, if not abjectly scarred.

The internship year continued. Right after the psychiatry rotation ended I faced my old, secret fear of the medical hospital and saw death up close again, many times. On the neurology service I rebelled against the dress code of white polyester pants and jacket. Despite an effort at stealth, my dark pants stood out vividly and I was taken to the side by the Chief, who told me to wear white or don't to bother show up. I went to Cozumel with some buddies for my sole vacation of the year. A hurricane blew in and it rained day and night. I gradually stopped using the loading dock and looking over my shoulder. It was, all told, a year of singular personal deprivation and stress.

I started my second year of residency in late June 1991, assigned to the sixth-floor resident unit. My entire residency class was glad to be done with internship and, like grateful parolees, we hit the units with hopefulness and fresh energy. After a year of fealty to multiple services across several hospitals, we were now all together. A camaraderie began that would last three years.

I'm not sure exactly when it started but, one day early in second year, I got the first call. I arrived home late one night and routinely hit the playback button on my answering machine. At first I thought it was a prank. The caller was red hot and unloaded a preamble of hateful profanity that would have made a longshoreman wince. What came next was a direct threat to my life and genitalia, in that order. To conclude, the caller shared that they knew where I lived, where I worked, and what I looked like. It was *Amanda*, no question. My gooseflesh confirmed it.

I did nothing after this call in the hope that she got it out of her system and it would be a one-shot deal. I hadn't seen or heard from Amanda in a year. The message was so over the top, to take it literally would have justified a bodyguard. It was a rant, I told myself. On the other hand I knew how disturbed Amanda could get, and what she was capable of physically. Just to play it safe I started looking over my shoulder again.

Alas, the calls did not stop. They came in randomly but always with the same motif—profane verbal abuse, threats to life and body parts. I began to save the recordings. I also informed my chief resident, the hospital administration, and security. After a handful of calls came in I said enough was enough, and the hospital filed a police report on my behalf.

The police could do nothing with the recordings; the caller did not identify herself so they could not act. "Call us if she attacks you" was their advice, which as you can imagine didn't do much for my sense of helplessness. In the beginning each call would lead me to redouble my street surveillance, but since I never ran into Amanda or her husband, as time went by the calls had less and less effect on me. It's amazing what one can get used to.

The year wove on. Between a full caseload on the unit, overnight call, and classes and supervision, my classmates and I became very busy very quickly. One of the places where you could run into a colleague and catch up was the mailroom. Payne Whitney, built in the 1930s, had a mailroom for staff in the lobby. Inside was a long wall with a giant honeycomb of small cubbies, each just big enough for letters. Every staff member had a single cubby for mail, which was placed in from behind by a hospital employee in the room on the other side of the wall.

One day mid-year I went to get my mail. My box was near the top row of cubbies, at eye level. I noticed a letter lying at a forty-five-degree angle in the box. The handwriting caused me to freeze. It was Amanda. I recognized her cursive from notes she had written that became part of her chart, notes that usually requested immediate release. The letter was too small to be a bomb so I took it out of the slot. No return address. It wasn't heavy but it bulged in the middle. That sent a wave of nausea through me. I put the letter back in the cubby and called security.

I tried to distract myself by returning to the action on the unit. A few hours later security paged me. They had clearly identified the contents of the envelope. It became obvious after sitting around their office a while. Excrement. Species indeterminate.

Amanda had stuffed the envelope with shit.

OK, this was getting out of hand. I had been a good sport with the death threats on the answering machine and accepted that no action could be taken. But Amanda's obsession with harassing me had crossed into the bizarre, and I worried what she would think of next. I marched to the chief resident's office and demanded the police be contacted again. From Amanda's letter we now had a handwriting sample that could identify her as the perpetrator.

Apparently handwriting analysis is something that is done in the movies or in very high-profile cases. I was neither. Another dead end; nothing could be done. I was flabbergasted that someone could be harassed to this surreal extent and have absolutely no legal recourse. That being said, my outrage was short-lived. The shit letter *was* kind of ridiculous, and I had sick patients to care for, a fact that put things into perspective every day. I received two more "special" envelopes from the shit lady, as she had become known around the hospital. By the third one, security, grown bored, threw it away without even bothering to open it.

In mid-winter things quieted down. The shit letters stopped and the phone messages became infrequent. Colleagues stopped asking me about Amanda at every encounter. My vigilance abated. I tried to focus on work.

Then, in early spring, Amanda released her next salvo. I received two letters from her, this time addressed to my home. One hand written and one typed, they contained the usual paranoid rants, but the second one had a new twist. It read as follows:

To: Daniel Mierlak

> Listen, you fucking extreme Racist Dog. If you value the use of you [sic] dick you will stop all harassing, and threatening calls, letters, & individuals having any contact with me.
> <u>FIRST & LAST CHANCE!</u>
> You Know Who!

She was accusing *me* of harassing *her* with calls and letters! What possible sensory information could she be distorting to arrive at this paranoid conclusion? Amanda's previous violence against staff, driven by a psychotic process, was at least based on interactions that *actually* happened. This threat to me made no sense whatsoever, and that was confusing, and scary.

I didn't have to demand a meeting after these letters came in. The affair had ascended to the highest levels of administration and *they* arranged a summit. I came with all the evidence I had, accompanied by the chief resident. He had been my main source of collegial support throughout this entire bizarre ordeal. The meeting was held in the office of the hospital's administrative chief. In addition to the chief and her number one, also in attendance was Dr. B., the department's expert in administrative psychiatry.

I reviewed the sordid affair from the beginning, especially the powerlessness I'd felt as each offense was met with a shrug of the shoulders from those in authority, including this very group of administrators. Once again they were sympathetic and promised to explore all possible options for remediation. In the years ahead I would work with this troika and discover that they were extremely effective professionals, and genuinely compassionate. At the moment though, I was wary of empty promises. Dr. B. suggested he take all of the materials and thoroughly study them as a first step. Feeling deferred, I left the meeting downcast.

Dr. B. was a gentle, soft-spoken, exceedingly level-headed psychiatrist. He was a national figure in administrative psychiatry, a field as dry as accounting. What I didn't know at the time was that, like accounting, administrative psychiatry selected for the meticulous and obsessional. Dr. B. sifted through the records like a prospector downstream from a gold mine. He too was perplexed by the change of content in Amanda's missives, from psychotic revenge for perceived past transgressions to psychotic rage at perceived current harassment.

Miraculously, he found an irregularity that could explain this shift. Amanda was being inappropriately billed for the ER visit that led to her admission in July. That ER stay should have been folded into the charges of the first hospital day. By some glitch she had been receiving a *separate* bill for that ER visit, a bill she wasn't paying. Dr. B. discovered that the unpaid bill triggered a collection agency action. *Voila*, the harassment! Nifty detective work.

Although it didn't explain her earlier threats, there was finally something that could be acted on. If the bill were made to go away, perhaps it would stop this latest obsession. I wanted to believe this. Administration shut down that charge and sent Amanda a lovely, contrite note of apology for the error, and assurance that the matter was ended.

The academic year was headed into the home stretch. My second-year class had become veterans of the inpatient service and we started to turn our attention to the third year, where we would inherit large outpatient caseloads and work the psych ER. As each week elapsed there was no contact from Amanda, no calls or letters. By mid-June it had been three months of silence. In the frenzy of preparing to transition from second to third year, the affair was all but forgotten. Dr. B.'s gambit had seemed to work. I was moving on to the next thing.

With only a few days left in second year I got paged to a strange number. It was the hospital's legal department; they asked me to come over. I walked to a part of the hospital complex doctors rarely visit. A document had been received from Amanda. She had not been silent these past months, rather she had changed tactics.

They showed me a summons, handwritten in a script I was all too familiar with. While the complaint, likely coached by legal counsel, was less psychotic than her other communications, it nevertheless rambled between civil rights violations, brain damage, falsification of records, government oppression, and the loss of her orgasm.

Amanda was suing the hospital, specifically the fourth-floor head nurse, the therapist she had accused of sexual advances, that person's MD backup (who happened to be my old chief resident), and me. The other three parties were being sued for $10 million each. Amanda and I, we were connected by a deeper bond.

Damages sought for my negligence: $25 million.

POSTSCRIPT

A New York State judge dismissed the case against all four of us, not on the merits, but because Amanda filed the complaint in the wrong court! The lawyers revealed that Amanda never attended any of the hearings; the scuttlebutt was she had moved back to Los Angeles. Amanda never contacted me again after the summons.

For the next ten years I had to check the "yes" box on official forms that asked if I'd ever been sued by a patient. That acknowledgment required an explanation of the circumstances behind the action. I would respond by simply attaching a copy of the judge's dismissal order; it was much easier than trying to explain the circumstances.

I didn't have a choice about taking this case since I was an intern, but I made a note to self for the future when I would have choice—*Maybe pass on patients who attack therapists.*

CASE TWO

THE LETTER

We stay inside the psychiatric hospital for our second case, which takes place in my second year of residency—a year spent entirely on the wards tending to individuals debilitated with the most serious episodes of psychiatric illness. The second-year psychiatry residents manage inpatient cases from soup to nuts, although, like all managers, they have superiors they must answer to.

This is a case of severe depression, in particular one of its most pernicious qualities—the phenomenon of hopelessness. A feeling that can afflict both the patient and the doctor, hopelessness contains within itself a fatal flaw—the perception that it will never change. How tragic this symptom can be in light of the powerful treatments we possess for the disease of depression.

> The sickest patients can challenge the psychiatrist's endurance to sit with the psychic pain of another.
>
> Sometimes the psychiatrist caves in.
>
> Sometimes the sickest patients get better.

I AWOKE INTO DARKNESS, INTO THE DEAD of night, to the high frequency chirps from my beeper, to my dyspepsia, and to my bad breath. Wrested from the elsewhere of my dream-life, the dreaded realization that I was in the on-call room of the Payne Whitney Clinic quickly coalesced around me.

The designation "Clinic" was an understatement and didn't do justice to the legacy of the Whitney family. The Payne Whitney Clinic was a nine-story, freestanding psychiatric hospital on the grounds of The New York Hospital complex, located within the patrician confines of Manhattan's Upper East Side. Built from pale granite during the Great Depression, in handsome deco style, the Clinic's rear façade abutted the FDR Drive and afforded priceless views of the East River and Roosevelt

Island. The institution was a heavyweight of American psychiatry, and for a kid from Queens whose parents grew up working fields in Belarus, to land a spot in its residency program was a coup.

Notwithstanding this venerable history, the on-call room—a Spartan cell slept in by a different psychiatry resident every night—felt more like a locker room with its layers of sweat-smell and utilitarian décor, and was best experienced asleep if possible. Well into my second year of residency training, I had endured many nights on call in the hospital. The abrupt arousal from deep stages of sleep produces a characteristic disquiet, like motion sickness. Unlike the civilian who gets a call in the middle of the night once in a blue moon, I had become proficient in shaking off the nausea of sleep disruption.

The sole physician on site for the overnight hours, I was responsible for the assessment of any medical or psychiatric questions that came up for patients hospitalized in the Clinic, and for admitting new patients who came to the emergency room with conditions that required treatment within the Clinic's wards. A couple of times a year a resident took call and slept through the night uninterrupted. This was not to be one of those lucky nights. But I had to remind myself nothing was as bad as last year's medicine rotation, where I could count on not sleeping *at all* every third night. Up in the Baker Tower during medicine I saw some of the most awful, beautiful sunrises.

As the beeper's LED confirmed, it was the emergency room calling. The third-year resident had decided someone needed admission. This particular patient had brought himself to the ER after a failed suicide attempt. He was a private patient of one of the senior faculty.

Third-year residents worked the ER in shifts, one during the day and another overnight. They assessed every person who came in and had the power to grant admission to the Clinic's inpatient units. The third years were sardonically classified based on their threshold for deciding who got into the hospital. Those who admitted few patients and protected their second-year comrades during call were "walls." Those with a hair trigger for admissions were "sieves." Admittedly, this self-serving assessment scheme had nothing to do with clinical care. (I was to learn next year that third years had a reciprocal classification system for the second years taking call in the hospital. It was very simple. We were just whiners or not.)

"Doing an admission" was the main thing second years did on call. In fact, call was almost always defined by how many one got:

1–2: easy night
3–4: rough night
5–6: brutal night
7–8: full moon
9+: legendary

Admissions were onerous and generally dreaded. The protocol was fairly standard. The third year initially phoned from the ER and then brought the patient up to the floor, where they presented the case more fully before running back downstairs. The second year then completely re-interviewed the patient, did a physical exam, wrote the admission note and admission orders, and discussed the case with nursing. Paradoxically, a night with four admissions could be psychologically benign—less time for anticipatory anxiety.

As in any endeavor, there were different approaches and styles to the admission exercise. Some residents focused on speed and boasted they could complete an admission door-to-door in under an hour. Others, knowing their admission note would be read aloud to the entire clinical team in the morning, took pains to do an exhaustive interview and write-up, an experience also painful to an already exhausted patient. Like a good contractor I strived to be neither the fastest nor slowest, and to include some cleverness in the note.

I threw on my tired pants and shirt, popped a mint, and went to the nurse's station. The third year wasn't in a mood to talk. The ER was busy and he needed to get back. That wasn't good news—more admissions were likely coming my way. As he scurried down the hall, the third year reiterated that this was a private patient of Dr. S., a senior faculty elite. The implication was clear—treat this as a VIP and don't cut corners.

Cooper was waiting for me in the unit's dining room. He had just been seen by nursing, who had among other procedures searched the small suitcase of clothing he brought with him to the ER. As I approached, Cooper's build suggested a linebacker some long time ago. Now, in middle age, Cooper was a large, overweight man, but his frame still exuded formidable physical strength. That's not what stood out though; it was the way he sat in the chair. Flaccid and exhausted, Cooper seemed to have come from battle. A battle lost. Defeat diffused out of him and filled the atmosphere of the room. If there were a contest for best iconic image of depression, this man would be a finalist.

"What brought you to the emergency room tonight, Mr. Cooper?" I began the interview.

Devoid of emotion, Cooper replied, "I held a Marine Corps killing knife to my chest for an hour, but couldn't plunge it in."

The way he said it, I had no doubt the man knew his way around a knife. Well, I certainly couldn't complain that the third year was a sieve on this one.

Cooper worked as a vice-president at a major pharmaceutical company. Depressed for years, his debility eventually prevented meaningful work and justified a full disability leave. He lived a solitary existence. Married once, Cooper's wife left him many years ago, and took their young daughter with her and disappeared. Cooper developed a single-minded dedication to the search for his daughter. After years of effort he located her, now a grown woman living in another state. He sent many letters entreating her to contact him but never received a reply. Until the other day, when Cooper got his first letter back. His daughter had written that she had no intention of *ever* meeting him, and implored him to stop writing. The letter was a cease and desist order. After he read her declaration, Cooper spent forty-eight hours in a convulsion of psychic agony, culminating in his moment of truth with the killing knife.

In psychiatric terminology, Cooper had what is called treatment-resistant depression. His symptoms—profound sadness, paralyzing lethargy, and all-consuming hopelessness—had not responded to trials of multiple medications. To make matters worse he was on an MAO inhibitor, considered by many to be the most powerful class of antidepressant medication, and was actually *getting worse*. The MAOIs were the end of the line in terms of antidepressants, and I wondered if Cooper knew that.

The interview concluded and we walked together to the physical examination room. At this hour, with the patients asleep and few staff on duty, the halls of the psychiatric hospital were eerie. The examination room, sparely furnished and far from the nurse's station, added some foreboding to the scene.

Cooper was not the kind of patient you chatted with during the physical. I wanted to get it over with quickly and return to the company of the staff. Cooper had taken off his shoes for the exam and at one point seemed to deliberately slide them under the examination table. I matter-of-factly bent down and picked up the shoes. A medium-sized switchblade slid into view.

I turned to Cooper, who was looking down, grim-faced and clenched. I guess he wanted to keep his options open in case we couldn't help him.

"We'll have to put this away," I said, and continued with the exam in silence.

Cooper had been assigned to my unit so I took him onto my personal caseload. In the morning, before I went home, Dr. S. came to the floor to discuss the treatment plan. He brought more bad news. Cooper had been seeing Dr. S. twice a week, at a top Manhattan fee covered 100% by his company, and was receiving full salary during the disability leave. This was all about to come to an end. The company would no longer provide these benefits. As a result, Dr. S. queried, it was not clear how Cooper would support himself after discharge. *"Wow,"* I thought, *"Dr. S. was able to imagine Cooper leaving the hospital."* I could not.

After a long and deep sleep the night post call, I returned to the unit and began regular sessions with my new patient. Cooper obsessively replayed the narrative of his family's life, seeking answers and absolution: Why had his wife abandoned him and taken away their child? What did he do to deserve that? He worked long hours yes, but only to provide a comfortable life for them. Did he neglect them? Maybe, but did that warrant her walking out?

It didn't add up. Cooper couldn't reconcile it. I nodded as Cooper went through the sequence, but I also wondered what he wasn't telling me about what went on in that family.

Cooper managed the blow of his wife's betrayal by projecting hope onto a future relationship with his daughter. She might still see him as a father who tried his best to support his family. If he had a chance to spend time with her, maybe she would see he didn't deserve the cruel fate meted by her mother. He had to cling to this possibility. Then came her letter. Cooper brought it with him to the hospital and shared it with me. The letter shattered his hopes, and worse, negated his past as father and husband. The long journey in search of reunion and redemption ended with the realization that, to his daughter, he was dead.

As I listened to Cooper's bleak ruminations an unpleasant heaviness beset my limbs. I shook that off, that feeling of being drawn into the hopelessness. Cooper would need more than medication or talk could offer, and that meant pulling out the big guns. For depression this severe, the treatment of choice was electroconvulsive therapy, aka "ECT," aka "shock treatment."

To the lay public, of all treatments in psychiatry, ECT remained cloaked in the most mystery. Patients rarely spoke openly of having received it, even if it saved their lives. There was no PR campaign by the profession to educate the public. As a result, ECT was largely misunderstood and feared. The vernacular "shock treatment" only made matters worse by conjuring up images of the snake pit. In actuality, ECT was safe, humane, and more effective for severe depression than antidepressant medication.

The therapeutic effects of epileptic convulsions in severe psychiatric illness have been known since at least the eighteenth century. Modern ECT developed as a treatment for depression decades ago, and is in essence a series of induced epileptic seizures. Patients are given "doses" of electricity, administered across electrodes applied to the scalp, until a grand mal seizure occurs. Over the years the procedure has evolved to greatly improve safety and comfort. The use of intravenous anesthetic and paralytic agents ensures that patients are both unconscious and unable to move during ECT.

The oft-cited fear of memory loss was overblown. Patients developed a lasting amnesia only for the time period around the ECT treatments themselves, a time usually worth forgetting. Stories of massive, permanent memory loss were the stuff of urban legend.

Cooper's medication was stopped and allowed to wash out of his body. ECT was administered Monday, Wednesday, and Friday. The treatments were done in a special room off a private hallway, in a secluded wing of the psychiatric hospital. The large room was dominated by a central table, like an operating theater, around which electronic equipment sat on carts.

His immediate responses to ECT were common and expected: a mild headache and grogginess, and amnesia for the period right before and after the procedure. After about six treatments he started to show signs of improvement: a little spontaneity, a little initiative. You had to know what to look for.

Around this time Dr. S., who hadn't been seen since admission, came to the unit and spoke to us in the nurse's station. He had apparently been deliberating and decided that, with the end to disability benefits imminent, Cooper in fact would not be able to afford to see him after the hospitalization. Therefore, Dr. S. announced, he was going to *unilaterally terminate the treatment now,* while Cooper was in a safe environment, and with enough time available for him to process this development and find a new outpatient psychiatrist.

Everyone in the nurse's station was taken aback by Dr. S.'s decision, but you couldn't tell from the response, because there wasn't any. No one asked Dr. S. the obvious question out loud—had he considered lowering his fee given the long relationship between the two of them? I figured he must have considered that but ultimately ruled it out. There was something in the way Dr. S. presented his rationale—he looked sheepish. Billing it *solely* as an economic reality didn't smell right. I couldn't help but feel that Dr. S. was burnt-out on this case, or maybe out of his league. Either way, S. wanted out.

Dr. S. met with his patient and broke the news. It concluded their two-year treatment. After he left I followed up quickly—and was surprised by Cooper's equanimity. I feared Dr. S.'s action would be experienced as a rejection and would rekindle the hopeless narrative that led to the suicide attempt. Instead, Cooper took the news in stride, and in the process revealed that his attachment to Dr. S. was more superficial than one might have predicted. Maybe they both wanted out.

The ECT marched forward. As the treatments increased in number the recovery time after each one grew longer—more hours feeling groggy and out of sorts, and an expansion of the amnesia to more hours before and after the treatments. This was completely normal. Cooper continued to slowly improve. His sleep, energy, and appetite corrected. He could be seen reading in the lounge and no longer filled the room with dread. He was not obsessed with speaking about his daughter. As a matter of fact he stopped referring to his quest to find her altogether, and instead spoke of his wish to return to work. Now, after weeks of ECT, I finally began to imagine that Cooper might recover enough to be discharged from the hospital.

It was during this period that, without much forethought, I brought up the daughter. It was a subject that had to be returned to eventually. Cooper responded by repeating the narrative I knew very well: details of his efforts to find her, his unanswered correspondence, etc. Something was missing though. The account ended just short of receiving her letter.

"What about the letter?" I asked without thinking.

Cooper looked puzzled at the question.

"What letter?"

POSTSCRIPT

Cooper forgot about his daughter's letter as a result of ECT that had gone on for weeks, yielding an amnesia that gradually oozed backwards to encompass the days immediately prior to admission. His lack of memory for it sent a shudder through me—I feared Cooper might re-experience a psychic collapse when reunited with the letter's harsh reality.

But because his depression had improved so much, Cooper's reaction to learning about the letter anew was appropriately sad but not cataclysmic. We went to his room together and found it among his belongings. Cooper's memory for the letter, and for all the details prior to his admission, returned before he left the hospital.

We found him a new psychiatrist in the neighborhood.

CASE THREE

THE MANILOW PARADOX

Let's take one last ride through the adventure park of inpatient psychiatry before we leave for the solitary confessional that is private practice. While it's assumed that the psychiatric hospital acts to contain the most peculiar expressions of pathology as regards the human mind, every so often even this assumption is not enough, as Case Three demonstrates.

Psychiatry is typically thought of as involving the interplay of two individuals, the doctor and the patient, much like singles tennis. In the psychiatric hospital however, the rules of the game, and the game itself, are less fixed, and occasionally one side chooses to play doubles.

Among medical residents, the slang "fascinoma" refers to a case of extreme rarity, something special seen maybe once in a career. To be close to the exceptional is often taken as a stroke of good luck.

In psychiatry, as you might expect, fascinomas carry their own nuance.

"HAS SHE MADE IT TO THE TUNNEL YET?" I asked myself, nervously eyeing the clock in the nurse's station. It was 4:20 p.m. The third-year psych resident in the ER had an admission, "an unusual case." She had called the unit at 4 p.m. to announce she was bringing the patient up. The inpatient units of the Payne Whitney Clinic were a long walk from the psych ER at New York Hospital, the second half of which was through a winding, Depression-era underground tunnel. I was the second-year resident up for the next admission on Payne Whitney 7, and I had a vested interest in the third year's arrival time.

For as long as anyone could remember, Payne Whitney had adopted a cutoff time of 4:30 p.m. to demark the deadline for daytime admissions. Any new patient who arrived onto the unit *before* 4:30 was the responsibility of the *unit* resident next in line for an admission. After 4:30, the on-call resident working the overnight would admit patients. The 4:30 line in the sand was sacrosanct, although there was ambiguity as to whether it referred to when the patient walked through the unit's door, or when the third year walked into the nurse's station. When patients arrived at 4:30 precisely, that lack of clarity led to heated debates.

It had been twenty minutes since the third year called from the ER. If I could make it ten more minutes I'd be free to go home when my work was finished, and would inherit the patient tomorrow morning, neatly processed and admitted by my on-call colleague. I was glued to the clock now—this one was going to be close. My heart sank when the third year walked into the station at 4:27. The admission was mine.

It was one of the swaggering third years. Only a year ahead in training but oh so far ahead in arrogance. Coming back to the hood to drop off an admission.

And what a prize to deliver. She blithely summarized the case, "Thirty-year-old deaf, mute, schizophrenic male with command hallucinations to kill himself." Hmm…schizophrenic patient, hallucinating voices telling him, *commanding him*, to kill himself. Can't hear. Can't speak. Wonderful. I relaxed. This was going to take a while so no reason to rush. My second-year colleagues in the nurse's station heard the summary and looked at me with sympathy. Inside though, I knew they were relieved to not get this trainwreck.

What they didn't appreciate was that I had a secret weapon: my medical student, Guy Russell. Guy was a rare find among Cornell students—both super smart *and* super efficient. Most medical students doubled a resident's workload because you had to explain *everything* to them. Not Guy though. He was a quick study, and more importantly, he had perfected the protocols of the admission process and actually *saved* time. Fortune shined on me twice with Guy, for he was also an excellent ultimate Frisbee player.

Ultimate Frisbee had become a bit of an obsession among a subgroup of us in the psychiatry residency program. The game allowed a bunch of cerebral shut-ins a way to flex their hyper-competitive muscles without jeopardizing their professional relationships. With his six-foot frame and Santa Monica forehand, Guy improved my team immeasurably, and therefore also enhanced my personal standing among the ultimate cognoscenti. With Guy at my side I knew we could bang out this admission, somehow.

The interview took place in my office. We had been told that the patient, named James, could lip-read. It was important to make sure the mouth wasn't obscured when speaking. James would write down responses to questions. The main narrative elements of his history came out in dramatic one-liners: "I became deaf at age eight after a virus," "The voices started when I was sixteen," "My parents were killed in a car crash when I was eighteen," "I've been homeless since then."

Presumably possessed of normal speech as a child, James should still have the capacity to make speech now even if he couldn't hear himself. Why he remained mute was a question we weren't going to touch at this moment.

A veteran of the psychiatric hospitals, James knew his way around the antipsychotic medications. Out in the world though, his medications invariably ran out or got lost and the voices would start up again. He heard a woman's voice instruct him to jump off a bridge or walk in front of a bus. Having enough insight to hear the insanity in those injunctions, James would take himself to an ER rather than act on the commands. There, the simple sentence, "I'm hearing voices telling me to kill myself," written on a scrap of paper and handed to a staff member, effectively put the institution in the position of gambling on the risk he might act on the psychotic directive. It would be a fool's bet to let him go, and so James would be admitted to psychiatry every time.

The psychiatric management of the case was straightforward. The antipsychotic medication was restarted and a waiting game for the voices to fade away began. The real problem was where to send him after he improved. A homeless person could not be discharged to the street. To find a housing option that would accept James could take a long time.

James garnered some notice within the hospital. "Hey, I heard you got the deaf schizophrenic with the voices." Granted, it did seem like an oxymoron, and those always get attention. But now, deep into my second year of residency, I'd gotten death threats from the disgruntled, mouth kisses from the manic, and heard an earful from the id. After the hoopla from the first couple of days settled down, James turned out to not be that interesting. With his housing placement the responsibility of the unit social worker, Guy and I moved on to our other cases.

Then one day, while I walked past the patients' common area, I heard the piano. It was an unusual occurrence, patients rarely played, and when I looked over I did a double take. My deaf patient was sitting at the piano, doing a serviceable job of an old standard. This incongruity caused a knot in my brow. It also bought James a session on the spot.

I grabbed Guy and we brought James into the office. How was he able to play the piano? James wrote that he taught himself to play some songs by ear as a child before he became deaf. Even though he couldn't hear the music he remembered the songs, and could see others enjoy his playing. Well, it certainly added to his allure on the unit. Perhaps there was more to James than I thought.

As the weeks passed and we waited for housing, a strange thing happened. Everyone stopped noticing James. He began to resemble the others—the other patients who weren't schizophrenic and who weren't deaf. One forgot James had a disability and a major psychotic illness. Maybe he was a great lip-reader and adapted remarkably to his hearing loss. But he was *also* schizophrenic, and seemed *too* related, *too* integrated into the culture and flow of the unit. Some staff spoke of James as an inspiration to have overcome this adversity. Guy and I were suspicious; he functioned too well. But with only a cynic's hunch to go on, we mostly just scratched our heads at it all.

The ultimate Frisbee was going very well. I tried not to think about Guy rotating off psychiatry in a few weeks. We were winning *now* and that's what mattered. Our field, on the North Meadow of Central Park, would get bathed by the voluptuous late afternoon Carnegie Hill light. That slanted magic light, combined with ultimate's sprint-induced endorphins, created a special bliss.

Then, one ordinary afternoon near the end of his rotation Guy burst into the nurse's station. He had been milling about the common area, where James had become a fixture on the piano. Guy was breathless.

"He's playing Manilow! *I Write the Songs*!"

"Barry Manilow? So?" I responded, blasé, not bothering to look up from my writing.

"It came out in '75!"

"So?" I managed, still distracted.

"He became deaf in '66!"

I turned at that and looked at him. *"So??"*

"He never took lessons, never learned to read music. *He shouldn't know it.*" Guy had that look on his face that you get when you know you've nailed something.

It took a few seconds for my brain to line up his data—when it did, it clicked like the tumblers in a lock cylinder. There was no doubt that Guy would become an exceptional doctor one day, but he could've also had a colorful career in law enforcement. Guy's deductions ripped into James' narrative of the case, and left behind a sloppy, jagged tear.

James was lying about being deaf. It was that or he lied about his ability to read music. Why would he lie about either? What else was he lying about? The suspicions that something didn't add up had just been confirmed, but they led to even more bewildering questions. We were pretty sure we were being played, but the nature of the play, the effort involved, was bizarre.

Feeling righteous, and a little wounded, Guy and I sat in the nurse's station and plotted a strategy to confront James, to see what he had to say for himself. The staff, gathered around as Guy's revelations were processed, would wait expectantly for the outcome of our intervention.

This time we interviewed James in his room. I began with a description of our observations of James in relation to how the illness of schizophrenia was understood, building up the sense of confusion we experienced. Then, using his own statements about how he learned to play the piano to create a denouement, I confronted James with the Manilow paradox.

James sat on the bed motionless for the entire explication. He made no move for paper or pen. Part of our strategy was to more carefully search James' belongings for information, hence the meeting in his room, and I told him we were going to do that now. Guy reached for James' wallet, which sat on a nearby desk.

What followed took maybe thirty seconds.

Startling us, just as Guy opened the billfold, James leapt from the bed. He grabbed the wallet from Guy, frantically hunted among the flaps, and produced a square piece of folded white paper. *Which he popped into his mouth and began chewing.*

I don't know which parts of the brain reconcile shock and disbelief, but it's safe to say they hadn't tackled anything like *this* before. Without time for conscious processing, and without any words spoken, Guy and I reflexively reached forward and stepped towards James. He slapped and shoved back with unexpected fury and, in an instant, we found ourselves each grabbing an arm to restrain the violence. James wrestled against us with surprising strength; the scuffle that ensued moved our interlocked forms toward the bed. He would not let up. The natural forces of struggle led us to lower James onto the mattress in an effort to improve our leverage.

James' options all but disappeared once he found himself lying on his back, held immobile by two men. He fought the hold nonetheless, but the work required, and the supine position, resulted in an unanticipated development—James started to gag on the wad of paper. Choking, his mouth now presented agape, and so I darted in with fingers and snatched the foreign body.

Once the parchment was retrieved James stopped his struggle and our hold was released. The three of us panted together for a minute. James became very angry and stopped cooperating completely. He gave us the silent treatment.

Heart rates still elevated, we returned to the nurse's station with the tattered evidence and replayed the episode for the rapt staff. The soggy document was unfolded and we discovered that the item held in such secrecy was an order form from a catalogue. A name, address, and phone number had been written in, but all was heavily painted over with Whiteout. Only two or three digits of the phone number could be discerned. I was crushed. A dead end. As the team tried to make sense of the clue, and of the Felliniesque scene that just transpired, Guy slipped away with the paper.

Clear headed in crisis, Guy speculated the correction fluid might be water-based and therefore dissolvable. With an archivist's touch he gently blotted the area with a wet paper towel, careful not to damage the underlying fibers.

Guy reappeared in the nurse's station a short while later, clutching the form overhead like Chamberlain returned from Munich. He had uncovered nine of the ten digits in the phone number. The area code was complete—it was a southeast city's exchange. With only one digit missing, I began to dial the ten possible phone number combinations, starting with zero and working up. My script was more or less the same for each call, "Hello, my name is doctor Dan Mierlak and I'm a psychiatrist from New York City. We found your number among a patient's belongings and we're trying to get some information."

I hit it on the third call—didn't even get past the first sentence.

After identifying myself as a psychiatrist, the tired, aged voice on the other end sighed, "Is he at it again?"

POSTSCRIPT

I had reached James' parents. They had not died in a car crash. James was not deaf and did not have schizophrenia. He had a psychiatric version of Munchausen's syndrome, which is a mental disorder whereby patients feign symptoms of a disease and undergo testing, hospitalization, even surgery sometimes. One of the curious features of Munchausen's syndrome is that there is no obvious personal gain from the deception, unlike, for example, a prisoner who might fake an illness to get out of his cell, or off a work detail. Perhaps there is a concealed personal gain in Munchausen's syndrome: by presenting oneself as sick, one gets cared for.

His parents revealed that James had been admitted to psychiatric hospitals across the south. They had received calls like mine before. They were baffled by their son's actions and asked him to come home many times, to no avail.

Once the behaviors are exposed, efforts to engage these patients in treatment are usually unsuccessful. Despite our offer to stay a bit and talk about his problem, the day after the intervention James asked to be released.

With nothing to leverage, we obliged him.

CASE FOUR

THE WORST CALL IN THE WORLD

When you start your career as a psychiatrist with the sickest patients in the psychiatric hospital, you might expect to feel relief in the shift to work with psychiatric outpatients. Actually, there is an unexpected anxiety which accompanies this switch. You realize that it's now you and the patient alone in your office—no colleagues nearby, or medical students—no attendings, no nurses, no security, no locked doors. *And*, here's the really scary part: the patient steps onto the street outside your office, free to do as they please with the contents of their mental life, *after every session*. Unsettling.

Case Four, which occurred early in the establishment of my private office, ably illustrates the risks of practicing outpatient psychiatry without the ropes and harnesses of the hospital unit. It also highlights a valuable talent that psychiatrists hope to refine over time: their intuition.

Episodes of depression, anxiety, and even psychosis, can be thought of as abnormal states that, when resolved, return patients to their baseline, customary personality.

The personality disorders are those conditions in which the baseline, customary personality **is itself** the abnormal state.

Within a given case, it can take a while for the psychiatrist to realize this distinction.

I WAS ON THE PHONE WITH THE 911 DISpatcher who, in contrast to my quavering delivery, remained very professional as I blurted, "I think a patient of mine has committed suicide." She kept me talking, and while we waited for the cruiser to arrive at Peter's address, her neutral diction calmed me a bit. After the police entered Peter's apartment I was patched into their radio communications. The policeman on the other end of the line was confused. He knew something was wrong—it just wasn't what he was expecting.

"Doc, I don't know what to tell ya. The guy's in a suit havin' a cup-a coffee. He says he's gettin' ready for a job interview." They gave Peter the radio. His rage exploded into my ear.

"What the fuck do you think you're doing!!? You're a fucking asshole, you know that!? I can't believe you called the fucking police, you fucking, stupid fuck…"

The pounding of my heart, which began when I called 911, now became complicated by another phenomenon: disorientation. Peter was not dead. He was on the phone, dressed in a suit, spewing verbal abuse. Standing beside him, the NYPD must have been embarrassed as they heard the profanity unleashed against his psychiatrist. Finally, mercifully, the cop took the radio back.

"Whaddya want us to do, Doc?" He sounded like he felt sorry for me. Head still spinning, I instructed them to take him to the hospital. When Peter heard that he erupted into another torrent of apoplexy. His screams faded as they led him away.

"You're fired!…You're fucking fired!…Do you hear me asshole?…You're fired!" The adrenaline took a long time to subside. No matter. I felt like an idiot.

This strange case had unfolded over a few short weeks. The initial call came from Evelyn, the director of HR for a large advertising agency. She had an employee who made a suicidal statement to some co-workers. A supervisor brought the employee to HR, where an interview resulted in his placement on immediate medical leave. He was told the company would arrange a psychiatric evaluation and would cover the cost for any treatment required. The company had a reputation for above average generosity in this regard. Evelyn gave me all the details she had and concluded her referral by pointing out something I knew was part of the deal—I would have to decide when the employee was safe to return to the workplace.

It was early in my career and I took it as a stroke of good luck that my name was in Evelyn's Rolodex. She worked for a brand name company that could become a source for future referrals. I needed to do a good job on this case.

Four days after Evelyn's call I met Peter in the office. He was a tall, muscular man in his mid-thirties. Casually dressed for the consultation, his meticulous grooming and crisp polo and khakis suggested a person who took his appearance seriously.

I started things off by explaining that I had two goals: to help Peter get treatment to feel better, and to help his company determine when he could return to work. It was important to be clear that this was a special situation. Because of the circumstances, Peter needed to understand that I would be in contact with HR about his fitness to return to work. I had discretion as to what to disclose of course, but the point was that Peter's discussions would not necessarily have complete confidentiality. He nodded his assent and then, in response to the first question, immediately got my attention.

"Monday afternoon I said I had enough with stuff in my life. I wanted to put a gun to my head."

I twitched, then squinted. "In a manner of speaking," he added, after a pause. Before I could respond, Peter launched into his problems.

For the past year he'd had headaches, fevers, seizures, and "partial paralysis." A CAT scan, initially read as brain cancer, terrified him. The follow-up MRI was clean. Despite extensive testing that repeatedly showed no pathology, he continued to have episodes of debilitating neurologic symptoms.

He was in a custody battle with his first wife over their child. His mother loved that grandchild, and when the divorce ended her connection, she blamed Peter and stopped speaking to him.

His second wife left him recently while he was sick. Peter began to suspect infidelity because of her inconsistent responses so he gave her an ultimatum: take care of me or leave. She left the next day.

This man was losing control—of his body, his marriage, his family. Peter offered that he was probably depressed and made a point to add that he detaches from his feelings. That was pretty clear—the interview was remarkable for the flat, bland narration of his recent calamities. I had heard more feeling at lectures on statistics. This self-asserted propensity to split off from emotions did not inspire confidence in my ability to read Peter's state of mind.

Although not entirely surprising, it did not help to discover Peter had virtually no social network. It was hard for him to let people get close. In what seemed sad, he cited his estranged wife as his main support. Peter weakly added his company as a source of support, namely the supervisor who brought him to HR.

A specific feature of the account tempered my reaction to Peter's circumstances: his seizures and paralysis *did not follow the rules of neuroanatomy*. They could not be due to biologically based dysfunction of brain circuits. They sounded more like *ataques de nervios*: fits of spastic writhing thought to be psychologically based responses to stress. At least he didn't have the misfortune of structural brain disease on top of all the rest. I was looking for any positive spin I could find.

Thankfully Peter denied feeling suicidal at the moment. He also confirmed he did not have access to firearms. Nevertheless, I was very concerned for his safety. Peter lit up the risk factors for suicide: a socially isolated male, separated from his main perceived support, hobbled by debilitating physical symptoms without known cause, depressed, and removed from his work.

I recommended he start an antidepressant. Peter certainly deserved one, but he balked. He just said no, he wasn't interested. And you have to trust me, despite the lack of modulation in his voice, there was a finality to his refusal.

So here was the first challenge: I'm sitting with an aloof, unreadable patient with massive stressors who recently told co-workers he wanted to blow his brains out, and he brushes off an antidepressant. I've formed little in the way of rapport, and the session is running late. I love this job.

Then it came to me. There was something in the way Peter spoke. I can't tell you exactly how, but the words, the tempo, and the timbre of his speech combined to exert a Svengali-like effect. Peter exuded a certain kind of, *intimidation*, for lack of a better word, that inhibited me from questioning or challenging him. This quality, as distinct an attribute as eye color, communicated without words, "There will be no discussion." It disarmed me.

Peter would not be swayed by argument; he had the advantage in that technique. So instead, I decided to find out what Peter was *willing* to do. I would take what Peter would give. He wasn't suicidal, so there was wiggle room. Peter agreed to stay with an aunt for a week and allowed me to contact his other doctors for information. It was best to double-check the medical details before declaring his seizures factitious. He also agreed to speak by phone daily and meet again in three days.

Communication proved problematic. Peter had disconnected his phone and his aunt had changed her number, so there were no phone check-ins. One doctor couldn't locate the records and the other didn't remember him, so there was no medical clarification.

He did show up for the first follow-up appointment. With no new information, I was back in the same spot I found myself in three days earlier, especially in regard to Peter's demeanor; he remained inscrutable. When I asked if he had any reactions to the initial visit, Peter responded with a single word, "Indifference."

Casually, Peter remarked that he wanted to return to work the next week. Sensing that my role was more likely to be bystander than counselor, I nevertheless had to weigh in on the request. I thought, "*What was the argument against going back to the office? He hadn't had any suicidal thoughts since his utterance at the job. Maybe that statement was just frustration blown out of proportion.*" Peter was depressed, but now that he was out of work he missed the structure, the routine, and the company of others. I took it as a good sign. Peter wanted to choose hope and action over resignation and withdrawal.

The desire to return to work afforded a bit of leverage. Peter would need my authorization, so I suggested he might want to reconsider the antidepressant Prozac now, as insurance against a flare up of depression in the office. Another incident there could raise questions about Peter's ability to remain in the work setting. Seeing the logic in this, and the self-interest, he agreed. It was a Friday. We were to meet again after the weekend.

Things did not go according to plan. Peter did not fill the prescription. Instead, he left town to attend the funeral of a cousin who died suddenly in Ohio. There and back in three days. Again, I found myself caught in

Peter's aural web. A funeral, even one in a different state, does not preclude medication. But the way he spun the tale, we diverted to a discussion on the tragic death of a relative rather than why he didn't get the medicine. Peter was in complete control of the narrative, and I felt like bringing up the failure to start Prozac would be rude, and disrespectful to the dead.

The talk of life and death and of extended family opened up some emotional terrain. Peter reflected on his difficulty trusting people. To make the point, he related a story about how he lived in a shelter at the beginning of his first job after college. His mother had reneged on her promise to cover his rent. The story was meant to explain why he kept everyone, including me, at arms-length. Peter had been burned by those closest to him. The account seemed improbable, but that deadpan delivery worked its magic again to shut me down. Finally, I grew tired of feeling impotent and I told Peter to start the Prozac, implying his clearance for work would be contingent.

Peter was back three days later, the morning of his return to the job. He was sharply dressed and, as I had come to expect, emotionally impenetrable. The first dose of Prozac had produced a nausea so complete, he spent the entire day in bed unable to function. When I asked why he hadn't called about the side effect, Peter replied, "What's the point?" The subsequent doses produced no problems. Otherwise, he felt no different, had no suicidal thoughts, and was ready to go to the office. We set up two sessions for the following week.

He was a no-show for both visits. His home phone was still disconnected and he didn't answer his work line. I started to suspect Peter was reasserting the upper hand by skipping out on the appointments. It was plausible. He had extracted the clearance to return to work. Perhaps he didn't need me any longer? Given how the treatment had been going that wouldn't be the worst thing. But I knew it wouldn't be that easy. I was a consultant for the company and they would undoubtedly want my feedback regarding Peter's mental health now that he was back at work.

As I contemplated my next move, I got a call from Evelyn. I hadn't spoken with her since the treatment began; I left a lengthy message the week prior about Peter's readiness to return to work. I assumed Evelyn wanted to talk in more detail about that message. I was wrong. That wasn't why Evelyn was calling.

Unbeknownst to me Peter was also referred to a psychologist after his comment about suicide. He had been seeing that therapist in parallel to the sessions with me, although he never mentioned it. Today the psychologist called HR to say Peter was more suicidal and should be hospitalized, and *that's* why Evelyn was calling.

I reached out directly to the psychologist; the call was quite illuminating. In addition to keeping us secret from each other, Peter had given us both very different versions of his history. It was as though we were discussing *two different patients*.

Peter's subterfuge had the immediate effect to toss his diagnosis of depression to the side of the road. In its place, his real disorder, was related to what I felt sitting in the room with him. At its heart Peter's pathology was in the nature of his interactions—interactions that, now exposed, sought to deceive and dominate.

It was of course Friday afternoon, the time when most difficult situations occur. The three actors in the patient's treatment (the psychologist, the director of HR, and I) had just realized they were bound together in a twisted plot written by the patient himself. I offered an intervention: to meet with Peter and Evelyn that afternoon. We would confront Peter about his deception and manipulation, possibly uncover his motive, and, more importantly, put an end to the drama. Evelyn would inform Peter about this mandatory meeting and bring him to my office, with security.

At 5:00 p.m., I opened the waiting room door to discover Evelyn and her security staff person. Peter, once again demonstrating who was in charge, had fled his building after getting wind of this appointment. We had our meeting anyway.

The exposure of Peter's deceit called into question *all* of the "facts" of his story. What was clear was the process that operated as a result of his actions: Peter mobilized alarm and action in *us*. Our natural instinct to help others, honed through years of training, was being manipulated. Perhaps that was Peter's motive all along—to feel the power of controlling us.

After we saw our reactions for what they were—the result of Peter playing with us like marionettes—Evelyn and I began to discount the seriousness of Peter's statements, in particular the ones he had made to the psychologist today. Neither of us was interested to have our strings tugged any further in the act of chasing him down, ostensibly to protect Peter from himself. We reinforced this sentiment for each other and concluded Peter wasn't a "real" suicide risk. We could just wait for him to surface next week. He would eventually show up at work, and we would eventually have our three-way conversation.

Another thing became clear in this meeting with Evelyn, namely the company's bottom line regarding what was expected of Peter upon his return to work. I had assumed that the company would see an employee who made a suicidal statement on the job as depressed, and would make improvement in the depression a condition for return to work. You can imagine I found it quite ironic to learn that, in the end, HR was less concerned with Peter's suicidality in the workplace than with whether I had addressed his *lateness and personal phone calls*.

In that moment the whole affair resolved, like the final scene from a farce: the stoic patient discovered to be an untreatable manipulator, the caring employer discovered to be clueless and banal, and the ardent psychiatrist discovered to be hapless and duped.

I was glad to have the weekend off from this case; I took it as an intermission. The performance would resume sometime next week. It was my habit to check my voicemail periodically during weekends, with the final check-in on Sunday evening before I went to sleep. For some reason that weekend I forgot Sunday night. I called in for messages Monday morning, upset with my neglect the night before. That's when I got Peter's call, the worst call, the call that sickened me and made me question what I thought I understood sixty hours earlier. Peter made it Sunday at 7:30 p.m.

The voicemail crackled into my ear, "By the time you hear this, I should be dead."

POSTSCRIPT

Peter's diagnosis was changed to antisocial personality disorder. Sometimes these patients are called sociopaths. They are thought to be inappropriate for psychotherapy that is based on the formation of a mutually respectful, non-exploitative relationship because they don't form those kinds of relationships.

When sociopathic behavior is discovered within therapy, or in any medical setting for that matter, it often elicits an angry response from the recipient. To be more precise, the emotional sequence is better characterized by shock first, quickly followed by hurt, which *then* slingshots into anger.

Healthcare workers assume patients act in good faith when they ask for help. When violated by a sociopathic patient, clinicians need to be on guard lest they drop this assumption for *future* patients.

The police did bring Peter to a local hospital as I had requested. He was admitted and then released a few days later.

Absurdly, he returned to work shortly thereafter, and, pragmatically, I found a way out of the case.

CASE FIVE

MY TIME IS GONNA COME

Few would dispute that psychiatrists ought to be experts at keeping secrets. Without discretion, arguably the whole enterprise of psychotherapy doesn't get off the ground. Yet there are times when a secret kept can seem at odds with a patient's best interest, as we see in Case Five.

This conflict is heightened when you've grown fond of your charge. The development of consequential attachments in patients towards their doctor has received more attention, but make no mistake that psychiatrists can manifest strong feelings in the reverse direction. I guess they don't call it a doctor-patient *relationship* for nothing.

> Confidentiality is a fundamental tenet for physicians, explicitly stated by Hippocrates in the 5th Century BC in his oath of ethics.
>
> It is a sacred covenant, for better or worse.

SOMEONE WAS LOOKING TO GET OUT OF a case and called their friend, Dr. E., who happened to be my supervisor. I had been in private supervision since the end of residency, a common professional practice. Dr. E. was a smart, talented psychiatrist with ten years of experience on me.

We met weekly, kind of like a therapy session, except instead of discussing my difficult personal situations, we discussed my difficult clinical situations. It was her idea I take this case; she thought I would be a good fit. Dr. E. described the patient: an early-thirties male, diagnosed with bipolar disorder and ADHD. He smoked marijuana daily, refused to take medications, and had a long history of behavioral problems. When she finished I scratched my head and thought, *"How did I become a good fit for this sort of case?"*

I fell for Jack immediately. He was a charismatic, infectiously optimistic character. Our initial sessions were a high-octane stream of (his) consciousness. He regaled me with his exploits and pratfalls, all delivered in a masterful manic style. Embedded within the extended stand-up Jack put forth was his history. By mentally cutting and pasting the offered vignettes, I began to discern the more linear narrative of Jack's life.

He was born into a prominent Boston family that drew its lineage back to the Mayflower. The expectation that Jack would one day assume the helm of the family business was dashed at an early age by the emergence of learning disorders and behavioral outbursts. These difficulties were so potent, they eventually overshadowed the positive attributes that resided within. To the outside world Jack was the hyperactive class clown with no impulse control. Impressive wealth and influence did not protect him from frequent afternoons in school administrators' offices. One by one, elite private schools from the Back Bay to the North End ran out of patience to manage Jack's *mishegas* and expelled him. The family's move to New York was strictly business, but it didn't hurt to have new educational opportunities.

By adolescence the mood swings of bipolar disorder were undeniable, and Jack became a mercurial hellion of opposition. He cast his parents as stodgy conservatives who responded to him by alternating between a shunning anger at his misbehavior and an iron-fisted need to pathologize and "fix" him. The latter orientation led to the offices of psychiatrists too many to count, beginning in early childhood, and resulted in a parade of diagnoses: attention deficit hyperactivity, oppositional defiance, antisocial personality disorder, substance abuse, and bipolar disorder.

What exactly did he want from therapy at this time? "You should talk to my parents," Jack answered.

So, I did. They had a lot to say, and they had a lot of opinions on what was wrong with Jack and what he, and I by extension, should be working on. As often happens when therapy involves two parties in conflict, I came to see that both camps had valid positions. His parents corroborated that Jack was a difficult kid with a long track record of troubles, but their pushiness also confirmed Jack's description of their less-than-ideal style of dealing with him.

The parents wanted me to keep their son out of trouble and they made it clear they were deeply invested in a biological origin to his problems. Jack was diagnosed by world-class psychiatrists as suffering from bipolar type 1 disorder, the most severe form of manic-depressive illness. He had had manic episodes in which his mood expanded to euphoria and he stopped sleeping for days. In this super-fueled state Jack would show up at their door at all hours, blathering a rapid-fire oratory of grandiose talents and plans, while they scrambled to contain him until the fit passed. On other occasions he would fall into a depression and hole up in his apartment, unreachable. Jack needed meds, but no one had been able to convince him to stay on anything for too long, and so the episodes kept recurring. "He must be medicated."

Then there was the marijuana. They scorned Jack's use and rightly worried about the role the drug played in his mood instability. It also contributed to his apathy they assumed, an apathy that led to numerous firings and evictions in the past. The parents worried about Jack's ability to live without squalor, to eat properly, and to engage in meaningful work. Marijuana was an obstacle to these things. "It must be stopped."

"*Very nice,*" I thought, "*now that the parents placed their order for their son, I just have to go into the kitchen and cook it up.*" I didn't share with them that in the sessions with Jack so far I felt like a spectator to a performance art piece. Jack certainly had a biological illness, but there was way more to him than that. He carried the weight of years of poor functioning and stigmatization, and I had no doubt his manic *personality* defended against deep shame and humiliation. "I'll do the best I can," I replied, and wondered what that would be worth in the end.

I brought the case into supervision, which was apt since Dr. E. brokered Jack's entry into my practice. She listened to me outline Jack's history, the sad tale of mental illness, opposition, and parental strong-arming. Through the supervisory work, I learned over the years the various and sometimes unexpected ways a psychiatrist could help a patient. After mulling over my presentation Dr. E. concluded, "He needs a strong, nonjudgmental male figure he can attach to and who he can trust as a voice of reason. Keep meeting with him." What about medication? "Sure," she added as an afterthought, "do what you can."

So I now had *two* road maps, one from the parents and one from Dr. E., and both had their place. The parents wanted me to be the doctor who medicated, and Dr. E. wanted me to be the therapist who became a surrogate parent. What was Jack's agenda though? What did he want?

"My parents said I have to come or no rent money."

Well, *that* was disappointing, but at least honest. I tried not to take it personally. Jack *was* coming in for the sessions, and that meant there could be opportunity for something to happen. I went back to basics: find out where the patient is coming from and try to form an alliance. During Jack's brief pauses for air I would quickly interject a question.

"What do you like about pot?"

Jack loved the high plain and simple, but he also felt marijuana was the only drug that helped his ADHD, the only thing that helped him focus and slow down his internal motor. If I thought he was a handful now, Jack argued, I should see him off pot.

"What about the stimulants?"

"Forget it, Doc."

The traditional stimulants for ADHD, drugs like Ritalin and Adderall, he summarily rejected. They were all tried in childhood and adolescence, and made his head feel packed with cotton and his body feel like it lost its gyroscope. These were deal-breaker side effects. Pot, on the other hand, helped him focus *and* felt good—a double positive. I told him I could understand that; I'd seen other patients who used pot similarly. But I also asked Jack to consider if there could be too much of a good thing, like when he got too high and skipped out on work. Could there be a way to smoke pot and stay functional? "It's food for thought."

During another session I was able to ask about the bipolar diagnosis. Jack properly understood the concept of bipolar as a mood disorder that could produce periods of abnormally euphoric or depressed moods, episodes that he had intimate familiarity with. Many mood-stabilizer medications had been prescribed for Jack since early childhood. He hated these drugs; they made him feel sedated and numb, and blunted his naturally "manic" baseline mood. That was something he couldn't risk. Jack's persona was *defined* by this zany, boundlessly energetic baseline. It was what the world *expected* of him, and he feared anything sedating would mute that baseline and therefore make him less interesting.

Now I understood Jack's willingness to suffer the occasional episode of severe manic or depressed mood—the trade-off for being unmedicated. It was an acceptable price to pay for the risk of becoming *ordinary*. Of course this was all based on the assumption that he was in fact less alluring on medication. "How do we know you're less interesting on mood stabilizers?"

The sessions inched forward. I mostly tried to understand Jack's perspectives and occasionally pointed out a trade-off to his decisions, and Jack mostly attended as required and occasionally considered my comments. Sometimes the consequences of Jack's behavior affected me personally and allowed direct feedback, like when he skipped sessions with excuses that were hard to believe. "Lying won't do much to help your cause."

I would be remiss as a psychiatrist if I didn't eventually get around to the reality that Jack was *under-functioning*, to put it mildly. He lived in his own apartment but he had no meaningful daytime structure. Jack's days were reserved for sleep, a result of nights spent festooned of pot and video games, with an occasional excursion to chase after girls. By all accounts his apartment was a rank chamber, as his mother feared. The long-term prospects for this lifestyle were dubious.

Financially, Jack was supported entirely by his parents, and whenever I mentioned this he became defensive and launched into a diatribe against their relentless intrusions, infantilizing actions, and pessimistic innuendo. I argued that by agreeing to this economic compact Jack fostered dependency on his parents, and then complained about not having autonomy. It was time to behave like a grown-up and start taking care of himself. If he couldn't do that, maybe his parents were right and he needed to be on meds. That got his attention; he said he would start looking for a job.

Another level of discussion as regards Jack's parents started to appear in the sessions. He confided that he had absolutely no interest or aptitude in finance or business—never even possessed a credit card—and felt his father was deeply disappointed to not have a male heir to succeed him in the family company. He suspected that was at the heart of why his father was so angry with him and rode him so hard. *I* suspected it was just one facet of the shame of having disabilities. His absence from the family business was never discussed explicitly of course, and so Jack wrestled with the pain of this filial failure by himself. "We should talk more about your relationship with your father."

The relationship with his mother had a different dynamic. Jack saw her need to control him as a product of her own anxiety. Her perpetual questions, double-checking, and stubborn devotion to behavioral rituals—"the policies" as Jack called them—served to reassure her, alas only for a moment, that the world would work the way she expected. It was a full-time job to live this way, to beat down every chance for spontaneity, and it made conversation, travel, and even a shared meal with her laborious to say the least. While Jack could identify with his mother's entrapment within symptoms, this insight wasn't enough to protect him from her provocations. Sensitized by years of exposure, it wouldn't take long for her staccato interrogations to set him off in a rage. "Maybe we can figure out some strategies to deal with your mother."

Jack eventually became comfortable enough with me that he started to share his dreams for the future. I learned that Jack was a writer and hoped to write a novel someday. He brimmed with ideas for projects and kept many journals, and he began to bring pieces in for me to read and review with him. Once he brought a bag filled with scraps of paper, each scribbled with a line or two he had written during sparks of creativity. To broaden his range, Jack asked that we begin a project together to identify new vocabulary words from the voluminous second edition Merriam-Webster dictionary I kept in the office. Prescience, *tabula rasa*, and tutelage, among others, made the list.

Jack's writings had some problems though. They were non-linear and scattered, like the digressive stream of consciousness when he got revved-up. It was difficult to discern a theme within the mass of his written material. Some of it was just gibberish, probably written when he had been manic. Jack could become downcast, and spoke at times of a writer's block and difficulty formulating his thoughts. Dejectedly, in those moments, he mused that there might be ways to live other than on the unstable edge of mania. We were back to that thorny place—the negative consequences of his untreated bipolar disorder. Sensing a new opportunity, and with the fresh meat of this writing deficit as incentive, I launched back into my stump speech for mood stabilizers. Jack shut me down again—no chance he would consider anything that could numb him.

And then one day he threw out a provocative statement, "Listen Doc, my life's not all fun and games." I asked him what he meant, but he shrugged me off.

Later, he dropped a few hints about some kind of internal experience of loneliness and despair. Finally I pressed him, "Look, what are you talking about?" And finally Jack answered, and in a matter of minutes changed everything.

He spoke in sentences but I heard him in fragments. Strange, sinister fragments: *"handed over to the government…experiments as a child…agents on the street…punishment for actions…"*

The actual narrative, in reconstruction, went like this:

> When he was a very young child, the government realized that Jack was born with an extraordinary gift: the power to influence world events with his mind. His parents were hoodwinked and turned him over to the authorities. He was subjected to horrible psychological and sexual torture by government agents, and then returned to his family to be raised as though nothing had happened. Jack still possessed his power to control world events, but the government sought to keep him in check by continuously monitoring his movements and conversations, and by sponsoring acts of retribution against the public for his misbehavior.

BOOM! An explosion occurred, and it was no comedy act. It was also not mania—Jack was dead serious. I had sat with Jack about four months. I had spoken with his parents about his past. I had conferred with the last psychiatrist who worked with him, Dr. E.'s friend. I had no idea. Neither did they. No one knew. Jack had spoken to no one about this, ever. And that's the way he wanted to keep it. First thing he said after he dropped the bombshell was that he didn't want his parents told.

That wasn't my immediate concern. I had a slew of questions ready to rattle off, but Jack wasn't particularly keen to answer them at the moment. He had apparently been carrying these beliefs for years, and whatever the reason he chose to share them with me now, sharing was the point. The secret was out, and that was enough for one session.

For me however, a breathtaking internal world had just been revealed and my psychiatrist inner voice screamed, *"This is psychosis! You've got to do something about this!"* But I looked at Jack, a few feet away, and I saw a calm patient. Jack possessed an outrageous parallel life in his mind, and it shocked to hear it for the first time, but for him this was a *chronic* situation. It didn't seem he had gotten into any serious trouble as a result of these beliefs. Jack was psychotic, but not dangerous. This was not an emergency. I didn't need to do anything right now. As far as the rest of the world was concerned, nothing had changed.

What I *did* do was high tail to Dr. E.'s office. What *was* emergent was my need for her help. For starters, I needed a witness to hear *my* account of *his* account. I literally needed to speak Jack's beliefs out loud to another person—they were so stunning I could not contain them myself. I also needed help to confirm my initial instincts and develop a plan forward.

Unruffled, Dr. E. listened to my agitated recount of the blow-by-blow. I finished with a deep sigh and looked to her. Dr. E. agreed Jack had likely been living with these beliefs secretly for years, and hadn't acted on them in any apparent harmful way. It was not an emergency of any safety sake, and it was not something acute that necessitated a hospitalization. There was time to plan a response.

"He trusts you. Keep fostering the alliance, leverage it to keep him out of trouble, and try to introduce meds over time." OK, that all made sense. "Oh, and he also needs you to act as a container for the delusions. They've probably become too much for him to bear alone." *Great.*

Jack had revealed the presence of a long-standing delusional disorder, which forced me to add another item to his bloated list of diagnoses. Delusions are fixed, false beliefs—ideas held onto with conviction despite evidence to the contrary—and are considered psychotic symptoms since they represent an inability to recognize reality. Delusional disorders are unusual among the chronic psychotic disorders in that patients can function well and appear appropriate as long as the delusional belief is not directly discussed. These strange maladies can go on quietly for decades, and are notoriously difficult to treat. First, they are obviously not conducive to persuasion, and second, they don't respond well to antipsychotic medications, the mainstay drugs for psychotic disorders.

There are several subtypes of delusional disorder. In the *erotomanic* type the delusion is that another person is in love with the patient. In the *jealous* type the patient has the delusional belief their romantic partner is unfaithful. Jack had a combination of the *grandiose* type (the belief in having a great talent or power) and the *persecutory* type (conviction of being experimented on, conspired against, etc.). He had a kind of partial insight into his delusions—he was convinced they were true but suspected no one would believe him, so he kept them quiet, until now.

The sessions continued after his blockbuster. Within our discussions Jack allowed a certain amount of time to flesh out the delusional material, then would pivot back to whatever issue needed attention: the girl he was interested in, the hunt for a job, the conflicts with his parents. I wanted to understand how Jack carried on with life while owning such a transcendent delusional system. In a way, the structure of our sessions revealed how he managed. Most of the time Jack simply maintained his routines without influence from the beliefs, just as when we talked about his usual concerns as though nothing was different. It was only when something happened that touched on the delusions, or when I brought them up directly, that Jack would be affected, for a time. By the following session the emotions raised by the confrontation had passed, and Jack was back to himself.

The parents had been calling me periodically, usually after an angry outburst at a family gathering or upon the suspicion Jack was high. I never let on about their son's psychosis; I remembered the discussions with Dr. E.: Jack had had this condition for many years…He wasn't acting in any dangerous way…He was entitled to confidentiality…There was time… I just needed to work to keep Jack out of trouble.

Gradually, more details emerged. The earliest elements of Jack's delusional system—the abuse while captive by the government—were the hardest to speak to. Jack's "memory" of the horrors was fuzzy and so painful to recall that he actively avoided my probes. Nevertheless, fragments of psychological and sexual manipulations, presumably to "break" him of his extrasensory power to influence events, were enough to paint a picture of an internal, anguished, institutional torture-scape. I stopped pushing him for more.

The "surveillance" phase began after Jack was returned to the family and still continued to this day. Two government agents, who he sarcastically dubbed Bill and Sam, had listened to his conversations and tailed him on the street for years, practically making careers out of his assignment. When not on a stakeout, Jack imagined they sat in a windowless office somewhere, leading dull lives while transcribing his actions from the cameras that recorded him. Now, years into this, he figured they turned off the consoles for long stretches out of a crushing boredom. Jack had humanized his spies into beleaguered civil servants who wore cheap suits and punched the clock, and counted down the years to when their government pensions would fund a retirement near a golf course.

It should be mentioned that Jack was invested in my embrace of his delusional beliefs. From the outset I had been very careful with my language so as to not overtly agree or refute Jack's claims. When he first pushed for an endorsement I feared if I didn't agree, Jack might leave treatment. So, I tiptoed around the question with comments like, "I can see how stressful it is to talk about this stuff." I was setting the stage for a medication pitch whose rationale would be to relieve symptoms of an understandable stress response. I did end up cornered to weigh in on the delusions a few times and gingerly expressed some uncertainty and skepticism. Jack became angry but ultimately found a way to tolerate my agnosticism, and then stopped asking for my imprimatur on the delusions altogether.

The interplay of grandiose and persecutory delusions began to take center stage. I noticed that Jack's belief in his ability to influence world affairs often took the form of his claiming credit for positive events, like when a criminal was apprehended or a record was set. Reciprocally, he had the delusional conviction that negative events, like accidents and assassinations, were government-sponsored retribution against him. These "retaliatory" acts always involved the death of innocents. Crashes and murders reported in the news were seen as *meant* for him, as "deniable killings" carried out by the government to punish him for using his powers. He became distraught after these news reports and took responsibility for these deaths. They wouldn't have happened if he didn't have his powers.

This was my opening to reintroduce the idea of medication. Jack became so upset after these incidents, it wasn't a stretch to pitch a med to reduce his distress. Still, despite the sickening reprisal delusions, he tended to bounce back after a few days and then string me along with empty promises. Once I conjectured that he was *obsessing* on these conspiracies and maybe Zyprexa, an antipsychotic with activity in severe obsessive-compulsive disorder, would help. I thought myself clever to come up with this angle to inveigle an antipsychotic into him, and even provided a scientific article to demonstrate the effect. Jack wouldn't bite.

Another approach was needed. I argued we spent too much time in an indulgent review of the past. We gave far too much attention to old forces from long ago. We needed to focus on the here and now as related to well-being and function. Jack wasn't making enough progress to take control of his life. He hadn't secured a job, changed his marijuana use, or cleaned his apartment. Whether through acceptance or detachment, or some other coping skill, Jack needed to move on from the past and address life in the present directly.

I knew I must have sounded like a fed-up parent, but I thought I had earned the right. Jack's response surprised me, and also made things clearer. Jack had no incentive to work the here and now because that wasn't necessary. You see, Jack was convinced he was up for a huge reward for his years of punishment. He was going to be taken care of finally—he was going to get payback, big time. The government would arrange it so Jack got a huge book deal from a major publishing house, and it was a sure thing it would be a bestseller, with others to follow. It was coming soon. He knew it. It had to be. He was *owed* it.

Jack dumped this new delusional data on me and then I had my own mini *aha!* moment. *Of course* Jack was passive and resistant. Why should he work on his life when he could just sit back and wait for his persecutors to decide, "Wow, we've put him through hell. He's suffered enough. Let's give him fame and fortune."

He expounded further. The government was to arrange the deal—one day he would get a cold call from a top tier publishing company offering him a contract. But make no mistake, Jack reassured, his writings would warrant the acclaim that followed: the readings, the signings, the radio interviews, and the book tours. His genius would be seen through the chaff, by the public and by the critics. The grandiose half of Jack's delusional world had been given a shot of steroids.

In psychotherapy, clarity can lead to complications. These new delusions cleared up my confusion about Jack's apparent self-defeating passivity, but they dimmed the prospects for moving him along the road to functionality. Jack humored me when implored to press the play button on his life. What did I have to offer, though? …a job as waiter?…as telemarketer?…hawking tickets for those double-decker tour buses? Feeble choices.

I took the chance to flex a more muscular skepticism against the conviction that Jack was going to get a free ride to the bestseller list, but it was to no avail. The belief was deeply set. Back and forth we went like fencers, parry and thrust, with no touches landing for either. Jack was stalling me, and his parents, who kept the heat up on the need for a job. The pressure from both sides started to get to him, and Jack responded by doubling down on the fantasy of a book deal. With each session the call of redemption from a publisher grew in urgency. He could feel it coming any day now, but as those days ticked by in silence, Jack's desperation grew.

It was during this crescendo of pressure and expectation that the first unraveling began.

A coincidence of tragedy—a powerful earthquake *and* a horrific bus crash in the same week, resulted in hundreds of victims. It was **them**. *But why?* He was on the verge of an end to the madness, and now this. Jack's emotional compass whipsawed from elated expectancy to a bludgeoning despair, and he reeled into an anguished spasm of survivor guilt.

Haunted by the victims who invaded his dream-life, Jack fell headlong into a deep depression. So close to salvation in his mind, the blow from this sadistic violence devastated him. The bastards didn't arrange the call with the book offer, rather they arranged carnage to further torture him. It took all of my leverage to get him to come to the office. Shattered and in disbelief, Jack broke down and wept for the dead. How could he be so wrong?

Here was another opening for medication but this time it wasn't about finding a clever tactic, this time I was worried about acute, severe depression. Thankfully, it didn't take any effort to secure his agreement. Jack had all the symptoms on the depression checklist, but it was the punch to the gut that made the difference.

"Give me the medicine, Doc," Jack now *demanded*.

I was prepared for this moment and had a medicine waiting in the wings. It was from a back shelf of psychiatry's medicine cabinet, an odd little concoction called Symbyax, the brainchild of some Eli Lilly executive. A simple hybrid of Prozac and Zyprexa, Symbyax combined the antidepressant I needed now (Prozac), with the antipsychotic I had wanted for some time (Zyprexa). It seemed the perfect choice.

The damn thing worked! He took the Symbyax on and off for three weeks, and by the end of that time the depression lifted. Gone was the despair—in its place Jack's natural cheerfulness returned. He cleaned himself up and started to go outside again. There is great relief after a serious bout of depression lifts, for patient *and* psychiatrist. When that glow began to ebb I noticed Jack wasn't obsessed with the book deal or the recent calamities in the world. Instead, he spoke of wanting to join a writer's workshop to hone his material, or maybe work with a coach. He thought he should move into a new apartment with a roommate. It would protect him from isolation, force him to stay tidy, and cost his parents less. This was more than I could have expected—Jack sounded realistic and responsible.

The next few months continued the trend. His creative energy returned. Jack became excited about a new project and devoted a set time to writing each day. He reconnected with some old friends, and networked for a job and a roommate. Isolated for so long, he had forgotten how much he enjoyed a circle of friends. For the first time I began to see Jack express a contentment that had some meat on the bone.

Sadly, it was within these encouraging developments that a second unraveling began.

It started behind the scenes. Jack stopped attending sessions and phoned instead—behavior I had seen from him before—so I wasn't laying eyes on him. He continued to assure all was well, and then went further to volunteer he felt freed from his oppressors. My initial excitement to hear this, a conclusive sign the delusions were receding, was short-lived. In place of persecution, Jack alluded to a burgeoning "creative awakening."

Something was askew—his mood was too sparkly, too expanded. He sounded souped-up, and the heightened creativity was not a good sign. I suspected Jack was *hypomanic*, which is an elevated mood state, but not at the level of full mania. I told him as much and said he needed to get on medication now or risk a progression into mania, which could lead to a loss of control that might land him in the hospital.

The boundary between hypomania and mania is difficult, if not impossible, to anticipate. Mania is usually an emergency situation that requires psychiatric hospitalization. Patients can become psychotic, disorganized, and unable to care for themselves. Hypomania is the runway to mania, a runway that can be very short, and needs to be medicated before take-off occurs. If Jack was hypomanic, I was now on the clock to get meds in him.

The point was moot. Jack rushed me off the phone after the mention of medication. A couple calls later and he finally answered, irate. He couldn't come in because it would make him late for an interview at Random House. That was it, Jack had crossed the line. I couldn't continue to stay involved remotely; he needed to come in to be assessed. He might already be at the point of needing hospitalization. I confronted Jack—by staying away from the office he made it impossible for me to treat him. The current arrangement could not continue. I threw everything I had into the kitchen sink, and added, as heavy-handed as I could muster, that he was putting me in a position where I couldn't guarantee his confidentiality.

It was too little, too late. Jack resolved the dilemma and fired me on the spot, slamming the phone down to seal the deal. All of our painstaking work together—especially, for me, the work to forge our therapeutic alliance—was all ultimately overmatched by mania and ended in a flash of anger on a phone call.

Out of options and flying blind, I had no choice now but to call Jack's parents and alert them to the incipient mania. I told them Jack had fired me, but also reassured them that my door was open if he agreed to come back.

Jack did end up hospitalized and, I was to learn, got a new psychiatrist.

After some time passed, I ambled over and shut the door.

POSTSCRIPT

When I looked back over the whole thing, the original roadmaps for treatment given by the parents and Dr. E. were *both* correct, but needed to work in tandem. Jack had to take medication regularly to stay out of trouble, this was painfully clear. However, the only way he would agree to that would be if he decided to trust someone's prescription *over* his mistrust of the medicines themselves. You could argue I had made some progress—Jack trusted me enough to disclose his delusions for the first time. In the end though, his mania beat me to the finish line. Perhaps the next psychiatrist would fare better to convince Jack to stay on a mood stabilizer and keep him out of trouble from the manic-depression.

I was confident Jack would recover from his mania; we have very good treatments for that. There was something I was less certain about—the question of whether Jack would share the existence of his delusional system with his new doctor. I had seen the places the delusions could take him to. I would never learn the answer to this question. No doctor ever contacted me after Jack left my practice, and I never did breach his confidentiality to his parents. But I thought about it every so often, especially when a patient said something that reminded me of Jack.

Years later, the question came up again in a moment that hit me like a two-by-four. It was when I stumbled upon Jack's obituary. It was a small entry, with no details as to cause of death, but it was the day Jack died that caused me to gasp.

The day after 9/11.

CASE SIX

GLASS OF WATER

The field of psychiatry has suffered more than its share of cynical appraisal. The pejorative claim that seeing a psychiatrist means you've lost your mind is false, not because it is incorrect, but because it is only partially true. Plenty of people are in their right mind *and* could do with some sessions.

At the same time, having heard the range of complaints from wary practitioners and disappointed patients alike, there is ample legitimate cynicism about psychiatry to go around. In Case Six, we confront some classic forms.

When you're early in your career as a psychiatrist and a former mentor calls with a referral, you take it. When that mentor says it's a special case and he thought of you specifically, you feel flattered.

You're firmly in mid-career when your reaction to that special referral, handpicked for you by an old boss, brushes right past flattery and into the realm of suspicion.

I RECEIVED A CALL FROM A FORMER teacher, an encouraging call. Dr. P. was about to retire and was dispersing his practice among colleagues, and needed a certain hand for a particular case—someone with the right kind of sensitivity. He had inherited the patient in question from his own mentor twenty years earlier, when that psychiatrist retired.

What attracted him to this case was difficult to see from the initial description. The patient was a *lifer*—a person who would need the support of a therapist forever. These patients usually carried a unique one-two punch: limited insight *and* limited functioning. What this meant in practice was they could frequently get into trouble, yet had a limited capacity to learn from their mistakes and adapt. Most therapists have a few of these cases, but since they can go on until someone moves or dies, one should be careful not to carry too many.

To sweeten the pot further this patient suffered from a severe mood disorder and had been hospitalized for psychosis. And the final "special" feature: he was seen for a token fee. Dr. P. was right, this patient would definitely need a clinician with a particular sensitivity.

I tried not to think of myself as a patsy. My relationship with Dr. P. had always been cordial. Dr. P. was clearly devoted to his patient; the effort to find a new psychiatrist seemed nothing but earnest. He knew my style and thought that would be the right fit. I should *want* to assume Dr. P.'s mantle, to sit with his patient, advise him on affairs, and keep him out of trouble. This was our work after all, wasn't it? I began to feel a little ashamed of my initial cynicism about the case. Dr. P. had been noble and resolute in treating his patient. He was the man's *physician*. I decided I would accept the case and try to carry on this tradition. It was the right thing to do. And besides, it was understood, I didn't really have much of a choice.

I ended up working with Barry for a decade. The transition was difficult and itself took a year. Barry was very attached to Dr. P. and idealized him. The dedication that I had assumed of Dr. P. was confirmed in Barry's account of their work together.

It didn't take long for me to discover why Dr. P. developed a strong attachment. Barry was a caring, gentle soul who, in many ways, had an ordinary life with ordinary problems, and who was grateful for the therapy. His mother died when he was young and he was raised an only child by a father who never remarried. He worked entry-level jobs and had conflicts with his bosses. He had a girlfriend and had issues around commitment. Over the years we talked about the things that happen in a person's life: conflicts, illness, and death in family and friends; firings, hirings, and managing bosses; anniversaries, graduations, and marriage. Barry eventually came to rely on me as he had Dr. P., and I in turn developed an affection for him.

One thing that never changed throughout the treatment was Barry's ability to speak volumes. He had a style replete with long, convoluted digressions and tangents that often left me lost in a maze of verbiage. I would attempt redirection towards anything that resembled a main point, in vain. The habit could not be broken. The negative interpersonal consequences of this behavior were easy to imagine.

To make matters worse, Barry repeated stories from his past *ad nauseam*. These stories were maddeningly detailed accounts of events he had attended, events whose import did not warrant such assiduous recitation. The reminiscences were remarkably stable over time, as though he repeated memorized passages from an incredibly boring biography. The frequency of his storytelling, and its utter lack of novelty, inflamed his girlfriend. At the first hint of one she would interrupt him, infuriated, and yell, "You're telling the stories again!" She could see them coming from a mile away.

To sit with Barry, the form and content of his language were formidable challenges for me as well. A third factor proved the game-changer. Barry produced speech in an absolutely hypnotic, nasal monotone. This oral delivery system, combined with tedious narration, would eventually bring me to my knees.

A difficult phase of the treatment was reached when I began to have trouble staying awake during the sessions. The monotone, which relentlessly droned Barry's entire narrative structure, was getting to me. I became so sensitized to its soporific effects that it did not matter what time of day we met, and trust me, I had shuffled Barry's appointment all around the calendar. Strangely, I exhibited no hint of sleepiness during the session prior or subsequent to Barry's. The monotone acted like a siren's song, drawing my EEG to Stage 1 sleep. I needed help.

Born out of this necessity I began an exploration of techniques to stay awake while seated. I had experienced this problem before at lifeless scientific conferences and at clinical rounds after rough nights on call. However, it was never as systematic as what I now faced, week in and week out.

I first tried an enormous container of hot coffee before Barry's session. No luck. I either became immune to caffeine or Barry's voice became its antidote. In any case, the only thing that worked to delay the slide down the slope of consciousness was the physical act of bringing the container to the mouth. You can't fall asleep if you're actively moving a part of your body. The impracticality of this technique for forty-five minutes becomes readily apparent. It might look less odd to dribble a basketball for the session.

Next, I remembered a tried and true maneuver first discovered by a friend during an exceptionally dull lecture in a small conference room. There is a bony ridge in the skull behind the ear. One can easily and discreetly jam a fingernail into this structure and self-inflict a stab of searing pain. While this can jolt the drowsy self into alertness, I discovered that the repetition required for my purpose could not be maintained.

I read somewhere that restlessness was a sign of fatigue. That seemed counter-intuitive until Barry's treatment. I could become remarkably fidgety in my chair, fighting hand-to-hand with sleep. The postures I struck at times looked ridiculous. And I always knew that these tormented flexions were signs that I was losing ground in the battle.

Prior to stumbling upon the only technique that reliably worked for this problem, I tried one other desperate measure. It was a bit more complicated. When I realized I was dangerously close to the precipice of sleep I simply interrupted Barry, stated I needed a glass of water, stood, and left the room. I would go to the bathroom, splash the coldest water available on my face, viciously berate myself for being weak, and then return. The session would pick up where it left off, none the wiser for the true motive of my brief recusal. This technique, which combined a sequence of physical actions with brutal self-deprecation, enjoyed early success.

There was a moment right before I fell full-asleep in the chair with Barry across from me. That moment was characterized by nothing. I had no idea that I was about to drop out of consciousness, dead in the water. There was no signal, no tip-off. What I *did* know was the feeling when my eyes snapped open: a brief squirt of adrenaline accompanied the horror of realizing that I *did* just fall asleep for an instant. I scanned Barry's face for a clue as to whether he observed my temporary vacancy. Seeing no obvious sign of detection, I relaxed, and breathed again.

Then Barry spoke, "Doctor, do you need a glass of water?"

POSTSCRIPT

The glass of water incident happened about two years into the treatment and it left me mortified. Barry was a good sport about it; he never discussed the gaffe beyond inquiring of my thirst that one time. I took that as his gift but was humbled by the breach, and realized a new technology was needed to solve this problem.

The physical maneuvers were ineffective, and also left open the risk of being detected over time, as the glass of water scandalously demonstrated. I needed a *mental* technique, something I could think about, something that could overcome the irresistible somnolence *and* be invisible.

The technique I stumbled upon, which proved incredibly reliable, was ridiculously simple.

During the session, while Barry spoke and I listened, in my mind's eye, I simultaneously visualized sex.

CASE SEVEN

THE BOSNIAN SURGEON

Among its many functionalities, the human mind is quite a good reasoning machine. Mentally, we are wired to connect dots. We can't help it. All day long we sort, collate, and interpret the varied streams of information that impinge on our subjective selves in order to make sense of the world.

As we see in Case Seven, an errant assumption, or faulty interpretation, can send lines of reasoning into bedeviled territories of causality and prediction. And, in case you haven't noticed yet, psychiatrists' minds have no special immunity from these natural predispositions.

The struggle to control one's own behavior in the face of psychiatric illness can be noble.

The struggle to control someone else's behavior can be terrifying.

TONY WAS DEALT A BAD HAND. THE SON of a violent, alcoholic father, he endured frequent beatings until late adolescence finally evened the playing field physically. There was no safe haven within the extended family. His paternal uncle's house was arguably worse—the abuse there drove Tony's cousin to suicide. Fear and pain fought a battle for dominance in Tony's environment, and in his mind. Fear won on both fronts.

Through indifference or irrelevance, Tony quit school in tenth grade. Then, with no prospects of his own design, he followed in his father's footsteps and became a chauffeur. He landed a plum job for a prominent family on Manhattan's gold coast. He'd been at it twenty-five years, attending to one of the richest families in the city.

The panic attacks began many years ago. They set upon him like seizures of internal electricity—the massive wad of adrenaline dumped into his bloodstream would render Tony terrified and incapacitated. In time the fear became self-sustaining, like the sun. Its agent, anxiety, infiltrated all conscious and unconscious spheres of his life: social discourse, occupational function, hopes for the future, his dream-life itself. All of these experiences did a first pass through anxiety. With no recourse available Tony again followed his father's example. Tapping into his genetic inheritance, Tony began aggressively drinking to quell the panic. Alcohol became his primary weapon against this enemy, and he wielded it expertly.

After a time, attributes long neglected or never acknowledged stirred within Tony and confronted the anxiety and drinking. He was a counterpuncher. He had curiosity. He could learn. Tony found a psychotherapist and started to talk. For years he applied himself to insight-oriented therapy, cognitive-behavioral therapy, and even philosophic inquiry. He became the student he never was: earnest, disciplined, intuitive. With these *new* weapons of insight and cognitive flexibility, Tony began to unwind the reflexive anxiety that embedded every experience.

His progress was remarkable; the anxiety loosened and receded. Then he stopped drinking alcohol altogether. By mastering anxiety through therapeutic work and determination, Tony's life began to proceed without filtration through fear. With one exception: his hands. They trembled in one specific circumstance—on the job, while holding the wheel. It wasn't clear whether his upper-crust clients registered the tell; they abhorred public awkwardness and would never remark on such a thing. Nevertheless, the suggestion that they were witnesses to his vulnerability weighed on him.

Tony spent years trying to solve the problem of this anxiety remnant, without success. As the pattern settled in, the tremulousness behind the wheel led to self-recriminations that gradually eroded the overall progress he worked so hard to achieve. Eventually, unable to prevail in this final campaign against anxiety, a heavy demoralization set in. Then, hopeless and depleted, he considered what had been for him unthinkable: medication. He got my name from his psychologist.

The first impression was formed in the waiting room. Wiry, and with perfectly coiffed hair, Tony grasped my offered hand with a deferential manner. In the office he provided the history described above. Tremor was the matter at hand. When it occurred, which Tony realized was when conversations with his passengers turned "personal," all else fell away. Tony would lock onto his trembling hands with a sickened dread. Cruelly Pavlovian, the conditioned fear of these encounters made his shaking all but a *fait accompli*. After work Tony would walk for hours in Central Park to wind down, or exercise to the point of exhaustion. He retreated from his social world. The tremor had become his sole focus, and with no visible progress, Tony was bereft. Testing for it in the office, I found the movements to be so fine as to be barely perceptible.

Perhaps because of his earlier regrettable use of alcohol, Tony felt all medicines for anxiety were a chemical cop-out. After some education to correct this misunderstanding, I suggested he try a beta-blocker, the treatment of choice for stage fright. The theory was sound—his anxiety could be seen as performance-based. The pill unfortunately did nothing for the tremor, but it did break his resistance to the idea of medication. Now open to biological options, Tony directly asked for a Plan B.

I went with a tranquilizer—pure, rapid, guaranteed anxiety relief. Some psychiatrists are skittish to prescribe tranquilizers, themselves potentially habit-forming, to patients with addiction histories. Tony's sustained abstinence from alcohol made me less wary, and given the degree to which the tremor had affected his life, I accepted that some risks might have to be taken. There was an immediate benefit. After some fiddling with the dose Tony came to report a consistent 60–70% improvement. Over the next year there was some slippage in the tranquilizer's effectiveness. I added a second drug, an anticonvulsant, and he regained a robust response. Tony's long war finally ended.

These two medications provided remarkably consistent results and would remain at stable, low doses for the next ten years. Tony had no appetite to tamper with the chemical formula that ended his misery. He was doing so well in fact, he suddenly stopped meeting with his psychologist. This happens occasionally, a patient abruptly ends a relationship with a therapist after medication resolves something the psychotherapy could not. I wondered how my psychologist colleagues felt when that happened to them. In this case I knew Tony's therapist well. She was a pro who supported whatever worked.

Over the next decade I saw Tony every six months for medication management. The tremor essentially disappeared and was not invoked again, except as an issue from the past. We spoke of other things after pacifying the anxiety, ordinary things like his career, his marriage, and his interests. Tony loved to travel and had amassed an impressive folio of international journeys.

During this time of excellent function, Tony began to mention a new fear, a fear that his hair was thinning. Seated across from him I didn't notice any difference, and confidently pronounced so. Deaf to these semi-annual assurances, Tony's preoccupation with hair grew, and it eventually became clear that thinning was, for him, irrefutable.

I understand that one's hair is a very important personal adornment. I daresay many of us have strong opinions about how our hair looks or should look— opinions that may be at odds with the consolations of others. To be fair, I did not examine Tony's hair. I did not assess its unit density over time. Perhaps it *was* thinning, even if not visible to me. Whatever the reality at the follicle level, Tony had become more distressed with the changes he perceived. He experimented with different hair cut styles and combing strategies. These would all be seen as unacceptable, and his frustration deepened.

It was in this unfortunate context that Tony appeared at his check-up one day and told me the story of how, during the past half year, he had consulted a surgeon in Bosnia to once and for all address the hair problem. I was surprised by this elaborate development; it seemed an extreme intervention. At the same time I knew Tony's tenacity, and with his fondness for exotic travel, I assumed Tony had researched an experimental treatment for hair restoration in the Balkans.

Sadly, he was dissatisfied with the outcome of the Bosnian procedure. It had to do with the part in his hair. It had gone askew as a result of the operation, something not obvious from my vantage point. As with the original complaint, I again found myself sitting across from Tony, unable to validate his anatomic observations.

Meeting every six months is a thin treatment to be sure. It is usually reserved for patients whose symptoms, medications, and circumstances are stable. Every once in a while though, a half-year comes along and throws you a curve. This session, not nearly long enough to process the unusual details, went by with the speed of a camera's flash, and was just as disorienting. In the end, fruitless to convince Tony that his part looked fine, we both finished unsettled. I thought about him later and tried to reassure myself, and imagined Tony would adjust to the part and his distress would fade, like the attitude towards a newly painted room whose color one initially disagrees with.

Six months later he returned wearing a baseball cap, visibly distraught. Surprising me again, Tony had traveled *back* to Bosnia after our last visit for a repair of the flawed first surgery. Apparently the surgeon agreed something was amiss and undertook a second, more extensive corrective operation. As Tony described it, the results were disastrous. The part was now hopelessly and irrevocably mangled, mangled to the point that no intervention, and he had tried them all, could coerce the hair to lie properly upon his pate. I asked him to remove the baseball cap. Something now *was* different about Tony's hair, but it was subtle and hard to describe.

Tony had worked up a good froth as he listed the cosmetic restrictions he had to contend with. Then, in a pivot I didn't foresee, his anger shifted to the Bosnian surgeon himself. How could this man, trained to repair these conditions, produce an outcome experienced as nothing short of disfigurement? Tony answered his own question. Malevolence. Only malevolence could reconcile the discrepancy. The Bosnian surgeon betrayed his oath to Hippocrates and deliberately defiled Tony's part, the surgical sadist. With these deductions in place his speech grew vengeful. Reaching its apogee, Tony's fury found an ancient cul de sac of the brain, the place where the ultimate wrongs are permanently righted: the domicile of homicide. With blood boiling and a look in the eyes to prove it, Tony spat out his wish to stalk and kill the Bosnian surgeon.

Festering unbeknownst to me, Tony's obsession had taken him to a very dark, distorted place. I needed to help him see this but there was another problem right now. Caught completely unaware, in a matter of minutes I found myself deep in a rabbit hole every psychiatrist fears: talking to a patient about their wish to kill another person. Tony was quite convincing. The Bosnian surgeon, this poor sod trying to carve out a niche for himself in Eastern Europe, certainly had made some serious mistakes in this case, but he obviously didn't deserve this reaction. I was freaking out inside and needed to get into damage control mode.

Tony could tell I was, *ahem*, unnerved. I tried to remember my training as a way to reset equilibrium: "...*assess seriousness, assess intention, assess plan, assess means...*" As I probed these questions Tony sensed my anxiety and backed off the murderous language. I remembered the concept of contracting and I asked Tony to agree to a contract that he would not, under any circumstance, act on urges to harm the surgeon. These sorts of contracts are usually of dubious guarantee, and are often cooked up by desperate clinicians hoping to bolster their own sense of control in the face of crisis. *Right, just like me!* Tony quickly agreed and defused some of the tension in the room. Despite his brisk assent I was still rattled to say the least, and continued to feel worried for the surgeon's safety.

"Perhaps we should meet sooner than six months," I suggested. "You're very upset and it's not good to have this much rage towards another person." Surely he deserved some more frequent sessions. Tony relaxed and sat back into the couch. He smiled. "Don't worry doctor. I'm not going to do anything. I don't want to get in any trouble."

He didn't want to come back earlier or more often. The original anxiety was under control and, in his mind, there was nothing else to discuss about the hair. That damage was done. I accepted that I would have to be satisfied with our contract for safety. *"All right,"* I thought, *"what the hell, ease up. You've got some time to sort this out."* After all, the Bosnian surgeon was 5,000 miles away from New York.

Like clockwork Tony was back in six months for his check-up. I steeled myself for this session—tensing the core to protect against a punch—because I realized a loose end had been left last time: I did not insist Tony *not* travel to Bosnia a third time. I knew the contract between us was flimsy; another trip to Bosnia would be too much. Were Tony to re-experience the homicidal rage I had seen in the office, while in proximity to the surgeon, it was unlikely he could control himself.

Thankfully Tony had not been back to Bosnia. As for everything else, nothing had changed. The part was still dreadfully off, he still blamed the surgeon, and he still wanted to kill. But he was measured about the whole thing, and his calm manner served to settle me down. Before any inquiry, Tony preempted me with unsolicited assurance that he posed no homicidal threat to the surgeon, undoubtedly remembering how shook up I was last time we met.

The session actually started to flow back to the old, familiar cadence we knew. I mulled to myself whether time would ever bleach the stain of this Bosnian affair on Tony's psyche. I suspected I would always take comfort knowing the surgeon was safely tucked away in Sarajevo, or some other God-forsaken corner of Bosnia.

During a pause, I mused out loud, "Well, at least the surgeon is in Bosnia."

Tony jerked with a start, surprised. "Bosnia?!" he exclaimed. "What are you talking about? The surgeon is at *Bosley*, on *39th street*."

POSTSCRIPT

After the follies of my rationales were exposed, and over time, Tony tapered his rage against the surgeon into a lasting, but thankfully more ordinary, grudge. We continued to meet every six months. Gradually the topic of Tony's hair drifted to a more distant orbit. In its place his old issues returned from their sabbatical. Tony eventually left my practice to see a doctor who took his insurance.

Years later he returned to me, explaining that the perfunctory sessions paid for by insurance were not worth the savings. His grievance towards the surgeon still quietly hummed in the background, muted and harmless. Tony's hair, though, had clearly taken a turn for the worse.

CASE EIGHT

WHAT IS THE HEROIN?

I became very interested to learn how to treat addicted patients soon after I established my private office, when I realized that, despite no mention of it initially, plenty of addicted patients *were already in my practice*. Addiction has an uncanny desire to stay hidden. Nevertheless, even in the most covert cases, the evidence seeps out, eventually…mostly.

The stories told of life subordinated to substances often contain elements of drama, tragedy, and farce, simultaneously. Not uncommonly, the narrative can strain credulity, as happens in Case Eight.

Like other guilds, mental health professionals use slang and sayings among themselves. One useful pearl is "When the treatment isn't working, reconsider the diagnosis."

Another favorite is "If you can't treat the patient, treat the family."

THE INITIAL CALL DID NOT SEEM PROMISING. On the voicemail, the man's Slavic accent was very thick. His name, and the name of the person who referred him, were unintelligible. I wrote his number down, an outer borough area code, and quickly forgot about it.

About a week later he called again, his message now conveying urgency and irritation. It was about his son, who apparently had a problem with heroin. Told I was the best doctor in New York for this kind of problem, the man pleaded for a call back. It was a situation I was familiar with.

I called him back and apologized for the delay. Mr. R. immediately adopted the deferential stance Eastern Europeans of his generation have for doctors. I did not recognize the name of the Russian physician who referred him—another feature of cases like this.

Mr. R. began to disjointedly outline the problems. Although only in his late teens, Sasha, his son, was already a career opiate addict with numerous treatments, arrests, and incarcerations to his credit.

Mr. R. wanted Sasha to be seen by an expert, this was clear. Much of the treatment and mayhem had taken place in Queens. He wanted to come to Manhattan to see a big shot who could fix Sasha. I was the best name he could find. I doubted I could be of much help but I now felt sorry for Mr. R., and since you never know what can happen in this business I agreed to meet them.

The initial greeting in the waiting room was not promising. Mr. R. sat alone and looked nervous. He was pure Eastern European immigrant: rumpled suit, five-o'clock shadow, thick neck, coarse hands. He explained that Sasha was in the bathroom. I invited him into the office. As we waited, Mr. R. clarified they were Ukrainian. It seemed it was just he and Sasha living together in Queens—there was no reference to Sasha's mother. He worked in the garment district but offered no specifics.

Again Mr. R. described the calamities that had rained down upon his son, and him by extension—the arrests for theft and possession, the cold turkey detoxes at Riker's, the numerous methadone programs that ended with Sasha getting kicked out.

And, of course, there was plenty of psychiatry as well. Sasha carried diagnoses of anxiety and depression and had been prescribed the usual culprits: antidepressants, tranquilizers, antipsychotics, and an anticonvulsant or two from the creative thinker who deduced bipolar disorder from the mélange.

Mr. R. was bewildered by all of it. He knew heroin was the enemy responsible for all the ravages. But why couldn't his son stay clean? He remembered Sasha, when not in the throes of addiction, as a kind, helpful young man. The methadone, the psych meds, the psych labels, these things he did not understand. Perhaps they were perpetuating the problem. He needed an expert to sort this out.

Twenty minutes had gone by and Sasha was still in the bathroom. Not promising. At last he appeared, less disheveled than expected—he must have shaved in the past day or two. He was skinny and looked exhausted. I asked Mr. R. to leave the office.

I dispensed with any illusion of taking a formal history and simply asked Sasha to explain his agenda for meeting today. It's not so easy to get this kind of information under these circumstances. There's a protocol that must be followed. It's like bargaining for a used car at the dealership. The salesman must first describe the hardship your offer entails, the anger he will engender from his manager, etc. Only after these stipulations will he reveal his initial price and then the negotiation can begin.

Sasha wove back and forth for ten minutes in this same dance. I dutifully nodded and asked the right questions to move the piece forward. Finally, Sasha complained that his methadone program wasn't taking his needs seriously.

"And what are these unmet needs?" I asked.

Then Sasha released his motive. "Anxiety," he said. Crippling, paralyzing, unremitting anxiety. He needed my help or it would surely be a return to the dope.

I paused to consider my next move. In a few seconds Sasha was out cold. Nodded out right there, right in front of me. Frozen in his last position. I woke him up.

"You just nodded out."

"I'm very tired."

Sasha resumed his complaints about the inadequacy of his treatment for anxiety. Apparently, anxiety was the source of all his problems. He wanted to know if I had any ideas to fix it. We discussed his current medications. The methadone program had put him on high dose methadone *and* high dose Xanax, but these were not touching the anxiety. I asked whether Sasha experienced extreme anxiety right at this moment. He replied yes.

I paused again, and again Sasha nodded out.

I invited Mr. R. back into the office. Sasha briefly roused. As Mr. R. and I spoke, Sasha nodded out yet again, unperturbed by the conversation. I explained that Sasha was overmedicated, and outlined a plan that was best implemented by the methadone program.

Mr. R. listened respectfully as I spoke. When I finished he looked down at the floor, processing the recommendations, I assumed. Then he looked up with a pained expression.

"Doctor, please to tell me, why does he like the heroin so much? What *is* the heroin?"

I thought for a moment. How could I convey to this man what this drug was? I landed on an analogy.

"Mr. R., you work in the city, right?"

"Yes."

"You take the subway every day from Queens, right?"

"Yes."

"Imagine one day you get picked up by a limo and get taken to work. The limo is huge, clean, with leather seats like couches. It has food, drinks, newspapers, whatever music you want. You go to work for weeks, months, in the limo. You get used to it. After a while you can't imagine taking the subway again. Inside, you know the limo is not really who you are, but you've gotten used to the limo and you don't want to give it up." I paused for dramatic effect.

"Heroin is like the limo."

Mr. R. followed every one of my words with fixed attention. There was a moment of silence, when I could see the wheels turning in his head. Then he spoke.

"I understand. Now I understand. Thank you, Doctor. Now I understand what is the heroin."

We sat together without speaking. It was a powerful moment. The father had gained some insight.

"Doctor, one more question. What is the methadone?"

Suddenly, Sasha stirred. He had been so immobile and quiet we had forgotten he was there. We both turned to him, this malnourished wretch, bent into an unnatural angle, bizarrely defying the laws of physics to remain seated.

Without opening his eyes, Sasha slurred, "Methadone is like the Long Island Railroad."

POSTSCRIPT

Notwithstanding poor public relations, methadone maintenance remains one of the most effective treatments for opioid addiction. Methadone is not a panacea of course and can be misused to get high. It also doesn't treat *other* chemical dependencies, and in this case one could argue Sasha had a Xanax dependency on top of an overuse of methadone.

Sasha's statement at the end might make one suspicious he misused methadone—it's better than the subway (ordinary life when not high), but not as good as a limo (heroin).

One more thing—never assume patients nodded out on opioids are asleep in the traditional sense.

CASE NINE

REVELATIONS

Colleagues outside of addiction psychiatry sometimes ask me how I can work with such a difficult population. I remember asking a medicine attending the same question when, as an intern on his bone marrow transplant service at Memorial Sloan Kettering Cancer Center, I rounded every day on those unfortunates whose transplants didn't take—those who would never regain their immunity, and who would never leave the hospital alive.

I say the same thing to my colleagues now that he said to me then, "You should come to my office and see the success stories!" Case Nine epitomizes the adage that after getting sober, addicts make great psychotherapy cases.

> The "aha! moment" is a well-known cliché in popular culture depictions of psychotherapy. While such moments do actually occur from time to time, one should not take for granted the implication that they induce lasting transformative change.
>
> But sometimes they do.

I WAS SEEING CLAIRE NOW ABOUT ONCE a month, but with the Christmas break, it had been two months since we last met. Claire was a medication patient, someone seen infrequently to monitor and manage her condition primarily through the biological lens of pharmaceuticals. I say *primarily through* because, as any seasoned psychiatrist knows, plenty of psychological material can emerge in "medication visits" if you're open to it, and see patients for more than fifteen minutes.

Claire was on Suboxone, a medicine to treat her opioid addiction. Suboxone had helped Claire stop the compulsive use of painkillers, an addiction that took over her thoughts and actions, and brought her to the brink of losing home, family, and career. After getting on the medicine she turned her life around and became a successful and respected lawyer. Claire's new identity as an esteemed professional was hard-fought and deserved, but also carried a secret vulnerability: would the addiction return if she got off Suboxone?

We had worked together for years, and the addiction went silent long ago. I encouraged Claire to try and wean off Suboxone many times. Her life had stabilized so much and for so long, maybe she didn't need it anymore. But it was never the right time. There was always something important going on professionally that couldn't risk any uncomfortable symptoms from the detox process.

A couple of times I convinced her to try a miniscule reduction of the Suboxone. Invariably something would happen: a little nausea, a little insomnia, a little restlessness. Claire would get scared and quickly snap back to her regular dose, and all would be well again. It was possible she had sensitivity to these tiny dose reductions. At the same time, we both suspected that fear of the unknown—life off Suboxone—was probably the real issue.

After we exchanged New Year's greetings Claire settled into a flustered expression. "I just got back from the worst weekend ever with my sister."

Over the years I had of course heard about Claire's childhood and family, but at this moment I had to admit I really didn't have much of a sense of her sister as a person, or her brother for that matter.

What I *did* know very well was that Claire experienced herself as the black sheep of the family. Both of her siblings, lawyers also, had excelled academically throughout all phases of their educational careers, right up to and including their prestigious law schools. As told from Claire's perspective, they were also goody two-shoes who never got into a stitch of trouble.

Claire's record, both academic and behavioral, had more variability and color. She was a streaky student who struggled at times, and although Claire ultimately completed law school it was clear within the family that she could only get into a mid-tier program. As a teen, Claire's choice of friends could extend to the sketchy, and she certainly experimented with sex, drugs, and rock 'n' roll, and got into the sorts of jams teenagers do. I never took her adolescence as too extreme or risky, but compared to her siblings you could see how Claire was cast as the wild one.

At times the discussions about her childhood revealed deep wounds. Claire had razor-sharp memories of humiliation by her father for poor grades or adolescent acting out. It didn't help that her father had started life as a welder's son in South Boston and hustled all the way to the top of an eight-figure business—a story she heard too many times. After years of disparagement, conspicuously absent for her siblings, Claire developed the idea that her family thought of her as stupid, lacking common sense, and ineffective. The achievement of a law degree seemed to provide little vindication. The addiction to painkillers, although kept secret from the family, threw gasoline on Claire's internal fire of shame and worthlessness. As she gained greater distance from the addiction and her legal career flourished, we spoke of these early memories less and less.

Claire didn't seem to begrudge her siblings, despite the chronic reminder that she failed to live up to their standards. But she also wasn't close with either. They all three lived in different cities, had their own families, saw little of each other, and spoke even less. They certainly didn't travel together, and that's what made the weekend with her sister unusual.

"What happened?"

"She's an insufferable chatterbox," Claire explained, and made the universal gesture for jabber by rapidly opening and closing her raised hand. "She takes up all the oxygen in the room. She literally cannot tolerate a moment of silence. On top of that, she's socially out to lunch…"

Claire described a series of distressing interactions from the weekend. She was clearly surprised and irritated by her sister's behavior. Her sister appeared to lack basic social skills in discretion, pushing conversations with strangers to inappropriate levels of familiarity, and exhibited infantile behaviors in public spaces. She also had unusual preferences regarding meals and sleep that she held onto with a vice-like rigidity, a rigidity itself notable and disconcerting. Her sister appeared to have no insight into the deviance of her actions and no recognition of Claire's cringes.

As Claire spoke about these behaviors an unexpected question formed in my mind, and without regard for its implications when she finished I asked, "Have you ever wondered if your sister is on the spectrum?"

I heard the gasp before I saw her eyes widen. She was momentarily stunned by the question. Claire's gaze became focused inward; I could see her rifling through the stored memories. I took the reaction as an affirmation.

"And her son," she added, still in a bit of a trance. After a pause, Claire went further.

"And my brother."

"And my father."

The data flooded out of her, disparate anecdotes and observations on Claire's nuclear family: the persistence of odd proclivities, the lack of enduring social relationships, the absence of humor, chronic social *faux pas*, professional setbacks, the rigidity, and the cluelessness—always the rigidity and cluelessness. The connections seemed obvious as she spoke, hidden in plain sight until now. Claire's father and siblings appeared high functioning to the outside world, but a closer look revealed they were *also* on the autism spectrum.

We sat silent, taking it all in. Then she started to cry.

"I'm confused. And scared. What does it mean about *me*? I can sound like my sister sometimes—I can say things the way she does. What if I have what she has and don't know it? What if others see it?"

After years of sessions it was clear to me Claire wasn't on the spectrum. But, since having a blind spot is part of the problem, Claire was panicked about whether she had a blind spot and couldn't see it.

"If you can ask these questions you don't have what they have." She started to settle down.

The shock from the realization about her father and siblings had an immediate impact on the story Claire had in her head about her place in the family. The harsh standard she was judged against throughout her childhood had just been discovered to be a distorted product of deeply limited individuals. That standard, and all its implications, had been turned upside down.

"All along they saw you as stupid, but in actuality, your 'deficit' *saved* you."

And just like that, the narrative of Claire's childhood was recast. *Poof.*

We spoke a bit longer and processed the fallout, both of us knowing a major reset had occurred. After she composed herself fully, I mentioned that I hadn't seen her this upset since the time she told me the story of being bullied in middle school.

"What was the name of that kid who bullied you? Joey something?"

"Johnny. Johnny Campo."

Several years earlier, Claire had shared the horrific saga of the systematic bullying at the hands of Johnny Campo. Despite no transgression against him, Johnny selected Claire for years of relentless humiliation at school and in the neighborhood. He was comprehensive in his cruelty and viciously taunted her when alone or in the presence of friends. Particularly savage was his musical serenade on the school bus, a pus-inspired hate speech sung to the tune of Bohemian Rhapsody, day in day out, while her sister sat beside her and, like all the others on the bus, did nothing.

As I recalled there was a redemptive end to the abuse, although my memory was spotty. "What was that thing that happened with your principal the day Johnny moved away?"

Claire began to retell the denouement of the Johnny Campo story.

Mercifully, Johnny's family made plans to move away, and Claire knew with that her torment would end. On the day Johnny left town Claire was euphoric—literally euphoric and feeling lighter of mass. It was a weekday and she found herself giddy as she moved through the school building that previously harbored dread. In this reverie she turned a corner into a long empty hallway. At the other end the principal likewise turned into the hallway. As they walked towards each other the principal paused momentarily, flipped a few switches on the wall that turned on some lights in the ceiling, and then kept walking. They passed each other midway without incident.

As Claire approached the far end of the hall with the switches, she was seized by a spasm of mischievousness and impulsively shut the lights the principal had just illuminated. He was now at the other end of the hallway, where she had started, but the change in lighting was undeniable. He wheeled around, saw Claire as the perpetrator, and yelled, a little too forcefully, "Stop!"

The disproportionate anger in his voice broke Claire's ecstatic stupor, and her internal state careened into a ditch. She was in big trouble, adrenaline bathed her organs, and Claire did what evolution destines all busted teenagers to do: she ran like hell. A chase through the hallways ensued. Claire kept her head and, assessing her options, implemented the terminal gambit to duck into the library, grab a seat at a carrel, and feign study.

The principal had his own adrenaline-fueled experience. He had morphed into a full-on Javert and, bursting into the library, rooted her out. Game over.

She was forcibly marched to his office, after a perp-walk through the library. There, his fury undiminished, he demanded to know why she turned the lights off. In a surprise move, Claire told the truth.

"I felt *big*," she said, "because Johnny Campo moved away today."

It was lost on him: the bullying, the helplessness, the humiliation, the reprieve, the euphoria, the emboldenment, the bolt of disobedience. Claire's impulsive defiance was misplaced no doubt, but the principal didn't know the back-story and therefore her action could only be misunderstood by this insecure, defensive little man. Her response to his question piqued no curiosity. Like a robot he concluded, "I'm going to have to call your parents."

That's as far as the Johnny Campo story had gone the first time she told me. Today, Claire went further. At home that night, she waited for the hammer to fall. Her mother brought her home from school and surely called her father at work with the news. He would mete out the discipline. Claire was a coiled spring at the dinner table with everyone gathered, but the incident was not brought up. Later, when her father was alone in the den, she was summoned.

In a ritual repeated since at least the 1950s, a father, reading in his den after a hard day's work, looked up from his newspaper to confront his misbehaved child.

"I heard you pulled the fire alarm."

Would that it had been so. Pulling the fire alarm, that iconic prank, was practically a rite of passage for any kid who fancied herself a risk taker. Not to mention the admiration it would stir among her classmates, especially if she got caught and carried herself with a bit of arrogance.

"No, it wasn't the fire alarm," she corrected. "I turned some lights off."

Claire went on to explain the affair: the walk down the hall, the principal who turned the lights on, impulsively shutting them off, the chase into the library. Her father listened, thought a second, and then asked the logical question, "Why did you do that?"

She repeated the truth, "I felt big because Johnny Campo moved away today."

I had been watching Claire intently as she recounted the coda of the Johnny Campo story. After this recollection she paused. Her face began to change: eyes narrowed, mouth quivering. She started to cry again.

"He laughed at me. He started laughing at me."

"He laughed at the story?" I offered.

"No. I wasn't laughing when I said it. He was laughing at *me*."

She kept crying as I tried to make sense of it. That day started so triumphantly. Her nemesis had gone away and she became free, free to live without fear. In her jubilation she made a mistake, and the aftermath of that mistake led her right back to humiliation, right back home.

It was a painful memory to share. After a time her tears slowed, and I broke the pall.

"I'm so sorry your father couldn't come through for you. Should have been a moment that made a father hug his kid."

"Yeah," Claire daubed at her eyes. "And it came out later that *all along* he had been fucking Johnny Campo's mother."

POSTSCRIPT

There were two revelations in this single session. The father's affair with Johnny's mother, an affair that started after the bullying began, was a revelation for *me*. I had questions at the ready, questions about how Claire reacted to this bombshell, but she was unmoved. It was just *one* of his affairs, she told me.

The discovery that Claire's father and siblings appeared to be on the autism spectrum, better described as having Asperger's Syndrome, was a revelation for us both. While it explained so much of the behavior of these three family members, Claire's strongest reaction was reserved for her father.

Interestingly, her father's history of philandering had not dented Claire's idealization of him as a successful, intelligent, worldly businessman who simply knew more about how everything worked than she did. The revelation about Asperger's, on the other hand, blew a massive hole in his credibility as expert and judge.

Claire's reaction towards her father after the revelation—fury over how she had been treated—was understandable, but his lack of insight into his disorder limited her options. Over time Claire's anger softened, and the revelation inspired her to adopt some useful, lasting changes.

In particular, the father gradually lost his authority over Claire, and, in its place, Claire gradually found the confidence to trust her own.

CASE TEN

MAKING MOVIES

Few psychiatrists make house calls anymore, if they ever did. That's a shame, because there's a blind spot in psychiatry, one that a good house call can shrink to a pinhole: the blind spot that, in the office, you only *hear* patients' versions of their lives. There's nothing like *seeing* someone's closets that gets to another kind of truth.

One must be cautious to attempt addiction psychiatry house calls though, as the risks are protean. It helps to have some aptitude in improvisational theater, as we see in Case Ten.

Psychiatrists in private practice often complain that their work is isolating.

On the other hand, there can be stress when one changes the environment.

THE MESSAGE, A SIMPLE DIRECTIVE, FORE-told a complex problem: "I think you better get down here."

I found myself in a cab, headed downtown to make the house call, trying to make sense of the voicemail message. Dixon, my homebound patient, was a well-known actor shooting a feature film in New York. His referral to me was temporary—for the duration of the project only. That was not a concern. Time-limited treatment has certain advantages, as any emergency room doctor can tell you.

Dixon's profession suggested an interesting treatment whatever the length.

Dixon had an issue in the past with cocaine, hence my involvement, and while that predilection posed potential complications, it actually was not a problem at the moment. The problem at the moment was that I wasn't seeing Dixon often enough to be of use to him, and, even more problematic, it wasn't clear how I *could* be of use. The film had a shooting schedule so brutal that Dixon often canceled, or simply didn't show up. I couldn't contact Dixon directly—that would be pointless since Dixon didn't control his schedule. Rather, everything went through his assistant. She seemed on the ball, but the film's shifting demands kept Dixon on location for days on end, and therefore mostly out of my office.

On the occasions when I did see Dixon, I saw a bereft man who was paid to play a movie star. Dixon hadn't had a day off or a proper night's sleep in six weeks, and that didn't take into account the long project he completed right before this film started shooting. Delays, rewrites, and retakes mired the work, and Dixon was out of gas.

There was more that weighed on Dixon than just long hours. His personal life was in a special kind of shambles—circumstances generally reserved for members of his exclusive club. His wife had filed for divorce and sought full custody of their kids. She was asking for an astronomical financial settlement, and she threatened to go public with the inside story of their life together: a life dominated by Dixon's drugging, gambling, sexual fetishism, and deep affiliation with cultist agendas. In between scenes Dixon spent hours on the phone in his trailer with a team of lawyers and PR crisis managers, trying to stay ahead of a vindictive spouse who smelled blood.

It didn't help that on set Dixon got little sympathy. Branded a tempestuous dilettante by the production staff, Dixon's scattershot scene schedule could put him outside half the night, and half-freezing, on the West Side Highway, followed by a 9 a.m. call on location in Queens. His efforts to petition for some efficiency were scoffed at and confirmed his reputation as a bad boy, probably due in part to the stream of impolitic profanity that colored the delivery of his suggestions.

There were other stressors as well, consequences of Dixon's formidable appetites, but you have enough to get the point. Dixon was cracking. He couldn't get the space to reset his mind or body. It was all work and all crisis, all the time. Dixon often lost it on set, blowing his lines with co-stars and blowing up with producers. All of it served to have the project fall further behind, with the effort to catch up leading to more mistakes and delays. It was a set-up for depression of course, and I had Dixon on medication, but I also saw that the schedule ground him down to pulp. All Dixon wanted was a break from work, which made a lot of sense.

There was no end in sight to the schedule though, and Dixon knew it. That put him in a predicament that always worried me: a patient who felt trapped. I asked all the logical questions a novice would about the shooting schedule of a major motion picture, looking for a seam to exploit. Dixon educated me on the film business and knocked down each naïve suggestion, and then left me with that hint of bile I got in the back of my throat when I sensed a no-win situation. I called Dixon's management team to solicit other options to reduce the shooting schedule, only to learn Dixon's assessment of the intractability was correct. Dixon *had* no options. He was on location every day for now, and all I saw was a man in a tunnel with no light.

At a loss to help him I in turn acquired Dixon's helplessness, and I didn't like the feeling one bit. Because I knew that feeling trapped and helpless could eventually lead to hopelessness.

And that could eventually lead to something rash.

I was in the taxi staring out the window, but my visual cortex registered nothing. Some other part of the brain was in charge and had commandeered all the synaptic chatter. It was that part of my brain that obsessively replayed dialogue, usually to no good end. For me, the internal process of compulsively repeating snippets of conversation typically served as self-condemnation for something stupid I imagined I had said, or, with equal recrimination, for some witty comeback I *failed* to have said. *Why did I never replay my clever bits?* In this moment though, I wasn't preoccupied with one of my "blunderances." My obsessional machinery had attached to the voicemail message. Dixon's assistant had left it an hour ago, and she wasn't answering my return calls.

I kept replaying her sentence in my head: *"I think you better get down here...I think you better get down here,"* and reworked the only things I had that could provide a clue to what was going on: her intonations, her inflections, her accenting. *What was her tone? Business-like? Serious? Urgent? Ominous?* **Ominous??** I worked hard to suppress the darker scenarios that inexorably formed on the outer edge of my consciousness.

The cab finally stopped in front of a non-descript, unmarked façade. No police—a good sign. I entered the "lobby," a sleek and uniform empty space that appeared functionless. As my eyes adjusted I noticed a hotel-like front desk made of stainless steel which, since identical to the surrounding walls, was near invisible. Behind this station stood a motionless figure, a handsome young man in an impeccably tailored slate-colored suit, also nearly invisible. As I approached the desk, I observed it held no paper, no console, no objects whatsoever. The attendant looked up. I stated the actor's name. The attendant looked to his right and said, "7-B." I walked to where he had gazed and a panel opened along the perimeter of the lobby—the elevator.

The assistant let me in. Dixon didn't live in New York and Seven-B, his temporary residence, was a furnished apartment that catered to the modernist hipster. The living room looked about as lived in as a room at the Royalton Hotel. The exchange of a few sentences with the assistant clarified that the worst had not befallen Dixon and immediately produced a noticeable relaxation in the musculature of my shoulders. With a cock of her head the assistant gestured down a hallway towards a bedroom. I could see the door was open so I gingerly walked into the empty chamber, like a nervous cop approaching a crime scene. The woman who had spent the night, or part of it at least, was long gone. There was water running in the en-suite bathroom.

The minimalist bedroom was all clean lines and right angles, except for one dramatic feature: the king-sized bed was savagely disheveled. Generous patches of powdered cocaine could be seen on the black sheets, as though someone shook baby powder willy-nilly. Dixon emerged from the bathroom. He looked like crap.

"Doc, I fucked up."

Wrung-out, Dixon slumped onto the bed and confessed his sins of the previous night. The testimony sobered him up a bit and as a result something else happened: Dixon became scared. He had missed this morning's shoot and that meant a hundred people showed up for work and stood around waiting for him. By noon, the train of dominoes that began to fall when Dixon let that woman in last night—they landed with a thud in the offices of the studio lawyers in Los Angeles.

He had fucked up all right. A lost day of shooting cost the studio a hell of a lot of money. Enough money that they had to know what happened, immediately: *Was he sick? If so, with what? When could he return to work? Or was it more sinister? Could he be counted on to continue the film?* I didn't let on that compared to the thoughts I had fended off in the cab, these questions were creampuffs.

Dixon told me that a protocol had already been initiated. A physician hired by the studio was en route to the apartment to examine him. There would also be a conference call with studio executives, lawyers, and his management team. It was imperative that he be allowed to return to work tomorrow. His contract had morality clauses. The truth, if it got out, would cost him dearly.

I looked around the bedroom and wondered how the truth could *not* come out.

On cue, Dr. Barrett, the studio doctor, dutifully arrived. As he was let in by the assistant, Dixon quickly shook and folded the bed sheet over in half, hiding the cocaine. Barrett introduced himself and stood in the doorway to the bedroom. "How you doing? You all right?"

Dixon sat on the bed, head down, dressed in t-shirt and boxers. "Yeah, yeah. I'm OK."

"You able to go back to work?"

"Yeah, sure."

"You're OK, right? You can go back to work tomorrow?"

"Yeah, definitely. Tomorrow."

"You sure? You don't look so good right now."

"Just exhausted from the schedule."

"Yeah, exhaustion. You should be fine by tomorrow." Barrett looked over to me. "He OK to return to work tomorrow?"

I had been standing off to the side observing the interaction between Barrett and Dixon, the three of us blocked out into a perfect equilateral triangle. I was unable to respond to Barrett immediately. There was a delay. I was working something out in my head that started when Barrett began his questions. My inner dialogue went something like this:

*"What in the hell is going on here…? Is he going to come into the room and examine Dixon…? No, I don't think he is… Is he going to ask about any specific symptom…? No, it doesn't look like he will… What the fuck **is** this…?"*

Both Dixon and Barrett now looked at me, waiting for my response. The pieces started to fit together, and I realized that the medical exam was a sham exercise that suited all parties. Barrett, shill for the studio, didn't want any details—didn't even want a blood pressure. He could see Dixon was not dead or disfigured and that was good enough for him and, presumably, for the studio. They didn't want questions or problems either, they just wanted performance. Dixon likewise didn't want any questions. He just wanted his sick day to raise as few red flags as possible and get back on location tomorrow.

"*OK,*" I thought, "*Let them play their game.*" I would talk to Dixon about the charade after Barrett left. My pause to process the absurdist scene must have lingered a bit too long for Barrett repeated, deadpan, "He OK to return to work tomorrow?"

I wouldn't bite at that directly. Looking at Barrett, I sidestepped, "That is his intention."

"Exhaustion," Barrett concluded after a pause—definitively and diagnostically.

He never did take one step into the bedroom.

After Barrett left to attend the conference call Dixon became considerably relieved. I did not.

"What the hell just happened here?"

"Welcome to my world, Doc."

Dixon confirmed that the studio wasn't interested in his health, just when he could come back to his role as stud horse for the movie. Barrett would report him exhausted but what would that mean? What would change? If Dixon and the studio agreed, the schedule would resume tomorrow, which would save Dixon's hide but leave an "exhausted" patient thrown right back into the fray. There's no business like show business.

As I puzzled on the Barrett interlude Dixon's manager called in. I assumed the conference call would wrap once Barrett gave the studio what it wanted.

I was wrong. Dixon's manager reached out to inform me that *I* was expected on the conference call, which was to start in ten minutes. I was being pulled further into the web.

Immediately Dixon sensed the implications and entreated me, "Doc, you can't tell them about the cocaine. You're my doctor and that's between you and me. You gotta get me back in tomorrow, Doc."

Briefly distracted by a caustic inner voice that berated my decision to hail that cab a couple hours ago, I nevertheless found the will to refocus. I looked at Dixon, who stared back with those puppy dog eyes. I was Dixon's doctor, that's correct, but I wasn't Dixon's *consigliere*.

"I'll get on the call if you want but what should I do if they directly ask me about drugs, lie?"

"Yes," Dixon reflexed.

What did I expect him to say?

It was quite a large conference call: studio lawyers and executives in Los Angeles, Dixon's representation (agent, lawyer, manager), local producers working on the film, Barrett, and me. After the introductions, the studio reps began by enumerating the absolute and relative financial outlays of the moneymen thus far. A biting analysis of the flawed shooting schedule, which culminated in today's lost work, was excruciatingly detailed in terms of financial and logistical costs and effectively shut up the local producers. This took about twenty minutes. Then came the first question regarding Dixon.

Barrett began to speak…the star was exhausted…but there was no serious medical issue…he was fit to return to work. Barrett was nothing if not reliable.

Who was this creature Barrett? I had not seen such a specimen before. *Did he have another job as a real doctor? How did Barrett get this gig? Did it pay well? How did Barrett calculate the liability risks of his doctoring?* Interesting questions I thought, but best left for a future circumspection, while idling at poolside, on holiday.

I had listened for the reaction from the cabal as they deliberated. Dixon's manager awkwardly chimed in and name-dropped other A-list actors who suffered similar exhaustive incidents on well-known films. No one seemed perturbed by his indiscretion. *"They really do see them as chattel,"* I concluded silently.

As the discussion progressed, a consensus was building to pick up with the normal schedule tomorrow. There was one voice from the Los Angeles contingent that clearly had authority. That executive eventually turned his attention to me, "OK listen, we have Dixon's psychiatrist on the phone. Dr. Mierlak, are you there?"

"Here it comes," I winced. "Yes, I'm here."

"Thank you for joining us. You've heard our discussion. Look, we understand you can't divulge any private information about your work with Dixon, but we'd like to know, if possible, if you think he can return to work tomorrow."

That's it? That's all you want?? You're not going to poke and prod inappropriately? I caught a break, an unexpected one, a break in the form of a big, fat softball. Glad to accept the offered gift, I replied, again obliquely, "Well, that is certainly what he would like to do."

Not surprisingly, the assemblage took my response as a vociferous yes. They started to gab start times and logistics. Dixon was going back on location and would avoid ruin, this time round. But what would happen the day after tomorrow? Everything was lining up to return to the way it had been the day before, including, it was a good bet to presume, Dixon's precarious state of mind. How would this help Dixon going forward?

I decided to ask. I cleared my throat and interrupted the gaggle, "Excuse me, is it possible to slow down the schedule so I could see Dixon more frequently? It might help him and maybe the project also."

With that there was a pause inside the conference call, a pause that lingered and raised a hopeful doubt. It didn't last long though. The money won out. They were far too behind to deliberately slow down. The full schedule would resume tomorrow. The exhaustion would have to be a one-day affliction.

Like eating a bad scallop.

When it was all over Dixon and I found ourselves in the kitchen. The assistant was gone; it was just the two of us. Dixon got his appetite back and started to take stuff out of a stocked refrigerator. Contrary to my reaction, he was not appalled by the behavior and outcome of the day's proceedings. It was just the business he said, and he expected no different. In fact, what Dixon felt was gratitude for he knew he had dodged a major bullet.

Somehow, Dixon got to talking about his childhood and the neighborhood he grew up in. Despite sitting in a kitchen, and following an unlikely afternoon's work, I reverted to a more conventional psychiatrist stance and drew out his memories and reflections. As he spoke, I realized that *my* early experiences weren't that far off from his. The dynamics of family, friends, and relationships have a universal language. And yet that surprised me as I thought about Dixon's persona as a movie star, packaged to seem otherworldly, inaccessible to ordinary citizens. How many people really knew him?

Now Dixon stood at the counter, still in boxers, working a slather of mayo into a slice of bread. He looked up from the cold cuts.

"Hey Doc, you want a sandwich?"

POSTSCRIPT

I continued to see Dixon for the remainder of the shoot. The studio did hear my concern; they eased up a bit and allowed Dixon more time to attend his sessions with me. Dixon stayed out of trouble following the house call. Eventually the project ended and we parted ways.

The film enjoyed some success.

CASE ELEVEN

THE ILLUSION OF DEPTH

That one would seek opportunities to alter consciousness makes complete sense to me. In its unaltered form consciousness is too often full of futile, pointless cognitions that increase unhappiness.

As a result, drugs, being quite reliable tools to change the "self," are understandably attractive. But why, as Case Eleven illustrates, do drugs sometimes deliver their gift at the cost of *unwanted* changes to *other* aspects of self, like self-control, self-care, and self-deception? Oh well, I suppose everything has its trade-offs.

The appearance of self-confidence gives one the advantage in many endeavors.

Especially sales.

HANDSOME, WELL-SPOKEN, AND WORKING two jobs while he prepared for the LSATs, Simon seemed the kind of kid who could accomplish whatever he put his mind to. And what Simon had in mind was to excel in law school and become a partner in a white-shoe firm. It didn't seem far-fetched; high achievement was a family affair. His three siblings had advanced degrees and both parents worked as engineers.

Simon was twenty-three years old, had the world at his fingertips, and was, incongruously, clean from Oxycontin for twenty-nine days.

Simon's parents brought him in; they were concerned. Their son had not revealed his addiction to painkillers with a tortured, tear-filled plea for help. Quite the contrary. Simon's addiction was *exposed*, and in the blandest fashion: via the discovery of a banking irregularity.

Unauthorized checks.

Simon's development of physical dependence to painkillers had followed a well-trodden path. Introduction to the encapsulated powder was brokered by a more experienced acquaintance. The first ingestion resulted in something Simon never experienced before: a unique, intense, and true euphoria. That euphoria, richly described through the ages, produced something else never experienced so comprehensively: a profound and irresistible wish to be repeated.

Initial indulgences were limited to weekends, like other recreations that separate work from play. But the memory of the drug's high could not be forgotten. It pushed itself unrelentingly to the top of the list of what Simon thought about, muscling past daily tasks and long held goals, compelling more and more opportunities for re-experience. As he used more frequently the physiologic dependence grew and eventually reached a tipping point, when nauseating physical withdrawal began to occur before day's end. Then, when he shortened the interval between doses to prevent getting sick, Simon eventually achieved daily, repetitive, compulsory use of the drug. It was a story I had heard so many times before, with such similar details, as to now sound like an Aesop's fable.

There was also a parallel psychological arc to the addiction. The habit began when Simon was in graduate school for engineering. As Simon's relationship with the drug strengthened, his relationship with humans weakened. He became introverted and withdrawn, and squandered friendships through neglect. He began to feel that he needed the drug to act at all. Simple tasks like leaving his apartment required a robust blood level of Oxycontin. This psychological dependence was not repaid with quality functioning. For the first time in his life Simon's grades plummeted and he was placed on academic probation. He stopped using after that indignity, shaken by the drug's ability to trash his semester, his GPA, and his savings.

Simon was at a crossroads, a "bottom" in 12-Step-speak. The pills had lured him into the carnival tent and performed an astonishing act of magic. What he cared about most in the world—success—had simply vanished from his repertoire of intentions. It was a bitter realization that should have humbled Simon, should have had him run to find help against this perverse enemy. It didn't. Simon wasn't practiced at humility. In large part pride, and in remainder a latent yearning for the pills, Simon just couldn't admit that addiction to the painkillers themselves was the primary problem. He needed something else to make sense of it, something fitting. He needed…*a villain.* A villain to pin it on. A villain so powerful that the daily, compulsive use of bankrupting sums of narcotics could be justified.

Simon found that villain in the concept of "the root cause"—the idea that a deep, hidden, fundamental conflict was active and unresolved, and was the real agent that drove behaviors like the gobbling of pills, injection of solutions, guzzling of spirits, etc. The root cause had to be profound in order to explain something as destructive as addiction. Heck, it might be so big that drug use could be seen as an understandable *self-medication* against the ravages of the "real" issue. In this wishful construction, addressing the root cause, whatever that was, would somehow trickle down and disempower the need to abuse painkillers. Of course the search for a root cause would *also* shift the focus away from the pills themselves, and while that misdirection might spare Simon's ego a bruise, if the theory were wrong it could prove costly.

It was during the break after this ruined semester that Simon discovered his root cause. It didn't take long to discern. Simon concluded that the *real* issue was engineering. Engineering wasn't what *he* wanted, it was what his *parents* wanted. He was in pursuit of the wrong degree; he was in the wrong graduate program. This wily deduction landed Simon squarely within the "I'm being forced to do something that isn't me" motif, just the kind of powerful intrapsychic conflict he needed to provide an ego-saving rationale to resort to drugs. The career mismatch represented by the "wrong" graduate program predicted a dreadful life, he posited, and could create a dissonance so intense as to easily be indicted as the source for the pill use. Or so the story would go. You had to give it to him, it was tight: simple, elegant, no loose ends. As a bonus, his reflections yielded clarity on what his *true* calling should be. Without a droplet of irony, it was during this period of reckoning that Simon realized he was destined to be a lawyer.

With this, Simon had sorted out the troubles of the past year. All he had to do was explain to his parents how the repugnance for engineering led to pills—and how he had decided to pursue law school instead—and he could begin his course correction. Another thing occurred to Simon as well. If he played it right, no one had to actually find out about the painkillers at all. Being in the "wrong" program, with all the chaos that that sowed in his psyche, could be enough to explain his poor grades. Surely his parents would understand the burden of all that internal dissonance. They would probably feel guilty for having suggested engineering in the first place. He could switch to law school and dodge the bullet of exposing his addiction. A double win.

But Simon didn't pull the trigger on his plan. Why? Because a terrible thing happened. The *thought* that he could keep the painkillers a *secret*, that they could remain concealed and he could still get out of his jam—the re-connection of pills with secrecy—well that created *possibility*. And possibility triggered a little voice within Simon, a voice that has wrecked many addicts, a crazy, irrational voice oblivious to his recent carnage, a voice that said, *"Hey, you can get high again."*

The craving was back. Its twisted logic concluded that since no one yet knew about the failed semester or the painkillers, he wasn't compelled to reveal *any* of it.

If Simon just kept his mouth shut he could go back to school and start using again. And so possibility found opportunity, and the game was done.

Of course his parents would eventually learn about the trashed semester, but this no longer concerned Simon. Only the wanting of the pills. The urge to get them took control of central command. Fantastically, on the verge of looping out of the addictive cycle, with a tidy face-saving strategy at the ready, Simon instead got whacked by a craving and collapsed back into the miasma. The root cause, freshly excavated from his imagination, and the brief resolve it spawned, were dispatched back to the shadows.

After the break Simon returned to school on a mission—sadly, it did not include academics. The Oxycontin came roaring back. The new habit easily broke the record for his previous personal best. Simon skipped the first day of classes and that was it, he never showed up at school again. Simon became a ghost, his days melded into each other in a disembodied narco-haze.

This manner of existence was, however sublime, not sustainable. From these depths of clandestine addiction, something eventually rises to the surface to uncloak the deceit. In Simon's case it was the bad checks, but it could also have been the disappearance from school, or from society, that eventually caught up with him.

His parents discovered the checking anomaly, asked their son a bewildered question about it, and then suffered a psychic concussion as he unloaded his two-year history of duplicity. Before the news could sink in Simon played the root cause card: that the whole thing would go away if he dropped engineering and started his prep for the LSATs. His parents wanted to believe this; it would be like waking up to realize the nightmare was only a dream. But they held onto a sliver of lucidity and insisted a medical opinion was needed to help them all decide what to do, and that's when the appointment with me was set up.

During the interval between getting busted by his parents and today's consultation, Simon arranged and completed his own detox from Oxycontin by procuring street Suboxone, a weaker prescription narcotic often used as a treatment for opioid addiction. Within Simon's cosmology, the end of the detox represented the literal *and* symbolic end of the addiction. The drug was now out of his body, and more importantly, it was also out of his mind. With his parents aware of the problem Simon found himself on a short leash, and the intense scrutiny had the effect to finally silence the little internal voice that schemed of ways to get high.

In this way he ended his story, the logic leading him to declare the addiction dead. Circumstances had conspired to break the spell of the painkillers, and he awoke ready to take action. Gone were the pills, the cravings, the conflict. In the month since discovery, Simon had dropped out of his engineering program, moved home, taken two part-time jobs, and started an LSAT course. Most important, he had made up his mind to stop using with ironclad certitude, and as far as he was concerned that ended the matter.

I followed Simon's self-possessed presentation of his history with a head-nodding straight face, one that mirrored his own. The penchant for addicted patients to relate remarkable events in a matter-of-fact fashion is not uncommon. It's as though adopting a tone of ordinariness to the narrative will make it so. I resisted my usual tells: a raised eyebrow, a squint. Instead, I interrupted at times and repeated out loud the unusual elements of Simon's story, in the hopes that it would lead to an acknowledgment of the unorthodox events. That didn't happen this time; Simon's defense couldn't be pierced.

I had spent the session listening, and occasionally repeating, and it was time I started to earn the other half of my fee. As I began to formulate my response it occurred to me that a good part of my work involved telling patients things they didn't want to hear.

Simon had earnestly served up his theory of cause and effect, and the recent "corrections" led him to think the addiction was over. However, it was naïve to presume the urge to take painkillers would simply fade away as a result of the changes he had made. For too long Simon had dealt with life's stressors, and banality, with painkillers. It was hard to imagine the provocations waiting for him wouldn't stir up the desire to call upon the pills. If that little inner voice returned, he would have nothing to fight back with. That's why he needed help.

I had to make my case carefully though. Simon might reject treatment if I implied too strongly that without it he would fail in the face of these challenges. This was a young man with formidable intellect, a past history of exceptional effectiveness, and an uncanny ability to discount the inconvenient.

So, with that in mind, in response I *complimented* Simon. Despite getting mixed up in an above-average addiction he didn't hurt himself irreparably, and he began his recovery with some smart choices, as well as a professional job of self-detox. Simon appeared pleased with my assessment. I went further: his parents would want to know what recommendations were made for situations like this, and he would probably have to agree to something to reassure them. He nodded as I spoke—Simon seemed to have anticipated this.

I was certain Simon had researched the treatment options but I dutifully reviewed them nonetheless. Inpatient rehab, the most intensive, restrictive, and expensive option, could be considered based on the severity of his addiction, but factors argued against it. First, the actual cycle of using the drug had stopped for several weeks, therefore a crisis rationale didn't apply. Second, he had never tried outpatient treatment, less restrictive and more affordable, so why not start there? After all, he had already put together nearly a month clean. Simon agreed without objection.

Next, I moved on to discuss the medications for narcotic addiction, biological tools I consider vital. Two molecules in particular act at opioid receptors in the brain and can interrupt compulsive drug use. One medicine, naltrexone, blocks the opioid receptor, so drugs like Oxycontin can't reach their target and produce a high. If you're on naltrexone and take Oxycontin, nothing happens, so compulsive use doesn't get off the ground. The other medicine, Suboxone, acts as a weak narcotic at the opioid receptor. Suboxone can be very helpful for patients who continue to experience strong cravings after completing detox. Many eventually succumb to these powerful urges and resume drug use. Suboxone can assuage cravings and thereby protect against this path to re-addiction.

Simon listened politely, and when I finished said no, he wouldn't be interested in either medication, thank you very much though. He preferred to address his addiction "drug-free."

The drug-free recovery movement always struck me as highly radical, and more than a little ironic given the massive doses of drugs self-administered without prejudice by addicted patients. This ideology confuses psychiatric and addiction medications with drugs of abuse, and by vilifying the former as vehemently as the latter, effectively throws the baby out with the bathwater.

Leaning into a well-worn shtick, I tried to correct his mistaken premise. Simon betrayed no irritation but firmly reasserted no interest in the medicines.

His body had had enough with contaminants. Things fared well so far with the all-natural approach. If that changed, if he felt vulnerable, he would consider one of the meds. I had been through these wars before and could tell this was an adversary I was not likely to persuade at this moment. I would have to accept Simon's concession to outpatient treatment as victory enough. I suggested we bring his parents in to finalize the recommendations.

Like the patient, the parents were calm and composed, a curious comportment given the fact that they had only recently learned their son had abused pills that could kill. It was hard to read their neutrality. Were they reassured by Simon's explanations for his addiction? Did they interpret his last few weeks of abstinence as the turnaround he predicted? When they articulated their intention—to learn what their son needed to do to address his problem—I still wondered whether they grasped the seriousness of his dependence.

Undeterred, I launched into a review of the options. The argument for outpatient treatment was repeated, with all in agreement. That part went smoothly.

Something gnawed at me though—and distracted me. It was Simon's rejection of the medicines. I just couldn't let that go. Unable to resist, I made another push for the addiction medications. Anticipating Simon's resistance I appealed directly to his parents, who almost certainly would agree to buy into some insurance for their son.

"He's been doing great the last couple weeks," I began, "and I know the medications represent putting chemicals back into the body, but why not use the blocker at least? It has no misuse risk and would offer peace of mind."

I touched a nerve. Before his parents could respond Simon spoke up, voice rising, galled with my back-door play.

"I don't want to put any other substances into my body!" he all but shouted at me, temporarily robbed of poise. The salvo preempted any input from his parents. They quickly capitulated, "OK, if that's what you're comfortable with, we'll do it that way."

In that interaction, the curtain on the power dynamics of this family, and arguably the consultation, had been pulled back.

I couldn't blame Simon for his rebuke. I had ignored his wishes regarding the meds and instead tried to enlist his parents to coerce him over to my position. I would've been pissed at that also.

Why was I so cynical about this kid? I scoffed at his root-cause theory, so amateurish, even though with other patients I'll think that kind of understanding is spot on. His plan for treatment I likewise dismissed as unsophisticated and imperiled. What button did Simon push in me?

I rummaged around in the bin of my Achilles heels and found it near the top. It was his brand of conceit. The kid came in with an I-know-how-I-got-addicted-and-I-know-how-to-stop *haughtiness*, much too thinly disguised by an exterior of *pseudo*-deference—and I don't like being trifled with that way. Simon had *no intention* of keeping an open mind to my opinions. He came to the consultation with his mind made up about how he got into this jam and how he was getting out of it. Outpatient rehab without medication assistance was the only option he would *ever* agree to.

Well, that certainly could explain my cynicism, but what if that was *my* problem? What if…Simon was right? What if, in *addition* to being a brat, he was right that outpatient rehab alone would be the best fit for him? At this point could I really be sure that I was interpreting the data correctly? Or did I skew it because I didn't like Simon's disrespect for my authority as a learned addiction psychiatrist? During residency a professor once told me, "When you're a consultant, they call you in to make recommendations, but they're not obliged to follow them." It's not so easy to keep an open mind, I suppose.

The room had become quiet again. I looked at the family and smiled, sincerely I hoped, "Very well then. We'll go with outpatient rehab."

We were at the end now. I was about to go over my preferred outpatient facilities when I saw the thing sitting in plain sight on the little side table nearby. It was the cup for the urine drug screen. I always had one handy, but during an initial evaluation there wasn't a set time I suggested we pause to do the test. I waited for an appropriate moment based on the flow of the conversation.

Testing for the presence of drugs of abuse is another oft-misunderstood tool in the armamentarium of addiction treatment. When derided by the uninitiated for conveying, *"You don't trust me,"* the true power of drug documentation is missed. Addicted patients in early recovery have a lot of trust to rebuild. Their actions, their speech, even their facial expressions, are often under the microscope of loved ones. These patients may have understandably engendered a bad reputation, but how should they respond to *erroneous* accusations of using drugs or being high? Impassioned denials of wrongdoing? That may sound all too familiar and carry no weight among loved ones who have been through the wringer. Now the power of drug testing becomes evident. Nothing silences the critics like a fresh, negative drug result. Once addicted patients grasp this simple equation, the drug test becomes a reliable friend, a credible ally who can vouch for trustworthiness about being clean. Of course one hopes that a lasting trust through proper action eventually triumphs and drug testing is no longer needed.

Without a flinch Simon took the cup and headed for the bathroom. Right there—the lack of hesitation on his part—I knew Simon was clean. His urine, a forceful ninety-four-degree flaxen-stream expelled from the bladder reservoir, would carry the historical record of any narcotic use over the past few days.

While Simon dealt with the specimen, his parents and I chatted about the differences between the outpatient centers recommended. They would do their own research as well, and probably have intakes at two different facilities before deciding which one to go with.

I was feeling better about the consultation. Simon's cooperativeness with the drug test softened the sting of his defiance. I reminded myself again that patients often know what they need. Simon's parents seemed pleased with the concept of outpatient rehab and were grateful for the heads up on where to look. It was all shaping up to end on a positive note.

Simon returned from the bathroom and placed the half-filled cup on the little side table. We spoke a bit longer as the testing chemicals percolated within his urine. The mood turned light; there was an unspoken hopefulness among us. The road back home for the patient and the family was in view. As they prepared to leave I felt comfortable enough that I made a small joke, and we all shared some welcome laughter.

I reached for the cup, which now seemed a perfunctory gesture. As I peeled back the tape to uncover the results, the slap to the face was mine alone for a moment. All ten drugs in the test kit were negative, double pink lines had formed in every column. Except the Oxycontin column. Its *single* pink line burned an undeniable positive result onto the side of the cup.

And it silently spoke to me, *"Schmuck…you had him right the first time."*

POSTSCRIPT

From years of work with addicted patients, I have learned the hard way that my ability to predict who will be successful is not reliable.

As a result I have decided that the best thing to do is avoid predictions altogether. Instead, it's better to clarify what patients want help with, work with them to achieve their goals, and point out when their actions create discrepancy.

For Simon, there was a pretty big discrepancy between his goals and his actions. What was truly deep was the skill with which he had become an expert in the double life.

After the urine result the parents sent Simon to inpatient rehab.

The truth eventually rises to the surface.

CASE TWELVE

THE LONGER YOU STAY

We conclude with a flashback—a very old med/psych case from internship. Typically, this would be a case involving a hospitalized medical patient who manifests symptoms that require psychiatric consultation. There is a unique subspecialty in psychiatry devoted to working with the medically ill.

Case Twelve is a different kind of med/psych case. It concerns the outcome of a chance encounter between two individuals—call one "med" and the other "psych"—who intersect on the inpatient medical service at New York Hospital. Let me be the first to disclose that the psych role here is played by your author.

> Lyrically, what more can be said about medical internship beyond that already written by Dante?
> *through me you enter into the city of woes*
> *through me you enter into eternal pain,*
> *through me you enter the population of loss.*
>
> Perhaps the poetry of Wilfred Owen:
> *If you could hear, at every jolt, the blood*
> *Come gargling from the froth-corrupted lungs,*
> *Obscene as cancer, bitter as the cud*
> *Of vile, incurable sores on innocent tongues...*

ONE GREY DAY ON THE MEDICINE ROTATION DURING internship, Mandy, my second-year resident, found me and said, "You're getting a DIC."

Mandy was a hardened, ruthlessly efficient technician in a pencil skirt and heels. Her subtlety appeared confined to the application of makeup. She had no discernible dynamic range of emotion when patients told their stories of illness. For Mandy it was simply question and answer, like taking a test.

Medicine was my second rotation of internship. I spent the first rotation on inpatient psychiatry, and although one could say I gained some valuable experience there, nevertheless, I had serious trepidation about transferring to a medical unit. It had to do with some unfinished business regarding a certain phobia of hospitals.

On the Friday prior to the switch to Medicine I had lunch with Rob, my colleague finishing up, whose service I would inherit. We met in the hospital's cafeteria. Our appearances formed quite a contrast. Coming over from the psychiatric hospital, I was dressed in low-budget business casual, rested from a rotation without overnight duty, and distinctly twitchy about what lay ahead for me. Rob had been up all night on call in the Baker tower, the massive minaret that housed the medical floors of New York Hospital. Dressed in pungent green scrubs, Rob was haggard and needed a shave, and distinctly euphoric over what was about to end for him. Come Monday morning, I would show up to Baker 16 and be the new intern responsible for Rob's patients.

The fact that I had never done this before created an unpleasant electrical sensation within me.

Rob began to summarize his patients, dropping medical jargon with an expert's nonchalance. The further he went, the greater the amperage flowed through me. He noticed my anxiety and, with an indifference that flew in the face of his future career as an empathic psychiatrist, simply affirmed that I was in for a brutal shock. After that truth was spoken, Rob's debrief on the patients failed to have any meaning for me.

All of my resources were diverted to the public management of fear.

Inside the hospital, in long hand notes and formal oral presentations, patients are identified as individuals of a certain age, marital status, race, and gender, who have a particular disease process. "Mr. Smith is a forty-five-year-old, single, Caucasian male admitted with pulmonary embolism." "Ms. Jones is a seventy-two-year-old, married, African-American female brought to the emergency room to rule-out myocardial infarction." In the short hand of the working medical unit though, patients are just their disease process. "Smith is the PE in 502." "Jones, the ROMI in the ER."

"You're getting a DIC."

After a fitful weekend in which I delicately applied an alcohol salve onto my anxiety, I arrived right on time to my new home on Baker 16. I sought out and introduced myself to Mandy. She would be my immediate boss and I her apprentice. She would teach me the clinical management of the medically ill. I would use her as my backstop to clarify questions and demonstrate procedures—my seasoned mentor. Mandy covered several interns but no matter, we shared my cases and together would collaborate on their care. The structure of the workday was straightforward: round on the patients, develop a clinical plan for the day, execute tasks. Mandy handed me a printout of my patients—names, room numbers, diagnoses, pending tests—and told me to round on them myself.

She had come in early and already finished her rounds.

DIC is an acronym for disseminated intravascular coagulation. In this dismal disorder, the body's clotting system goes haywire. One particularly nasty version of this disease has small blood clots form, not normally as in response to a cut in the skin, but instead spontaneously within the arteries of the circulatory system. These small clots race forward in the arterial slipstream, along ever-narrowing plumbing, until they become wedged and form a complete blockage of the vessel. Mayhem ensues.

Losing its blood supply of oxygen, everything on the far side of the blockage dies a slow, gangrenous death.

At the nurse's station, I sized up the chart rack. It seemed perfectly natural to review one chart, see that patient and write their note, organize their clinical tasks for the day, and then move on to the next patient. By 6 p.m., halfway through my roster, I noticed the other interns signing out their caseloads to the overnight team, their day's work done. A discreet inquiry revealed that these interns rounded on their patients *en masse*, wrote all their notes in one sitting, and then furiously completed their day's tasks and signed out as early as decorum allowed. I couldn't get to the end of my work list because, as long as I was on the unit, nursing would come to *me* with any new questions or problems on my patients. The boat was leaking faster than I could bail. It was one of the immutable laws of internship:

The longer you stay...*the longer you stay.*

On that grey day, there was a queasy buzz in the nurse's station on Baker 16. Matt, our third year uberresident, was in a bad mood. He had just lost a power play to his counterpart in the medical intensive care unit. It was the DIC. She was being transferred to us from another hospital ill equipped to handle her complex care. Smelling a very sick admission, Matt attempted to divert the transfer. He crafted an argument worthy of a solicitor general beseeching the patient's admission to ICU. The third year resident responsible for the medical ICU, Matt's colleague, had veto power over his peers when it came to requests for ICU admission. He refused to accept the patient. Matt's gambit failed. The DIC was coming to us, the nurses were skittish, and I was up for the next admission. I poked around a bit and learned that the patient had a gruesome form of the disease.

She had had multiple clots end their journey in her extremities, resulting in the amputation of parts of both arms and both legs.

Internship is a year of deprivation. Sleep, exercise, nutrition, relationships, leisure, the outside world itself—all are subordinated to the needs of the hospital. Take a typical medicine rotation with call every third night. On the day of call, interns work all day and likely stay up all night tending to the floor. The next day they don't leave until they've completed their rounds and prepared their patients for the day's tests. If they get out late morning they've done well. The rest of the day is shot. I usually fell asleep on the subway home to Park Slope. When I finally emerged to the street, vole-like, the short walk home was a dysphoric stupor, followed by a dreamless, non-credible recovery sleep. The third day was deceptively ordinary: rounds in the morning, work, and out by 6:00 p.m. barring disaster. Then the Stygian cycle starts again, and repeats over and over, paying no heed to weekends or holidays.

Work and sleep.

*The specter of bearing witness to her body, surgically devolving into a torso as it was, sent that electrical fear through me. I knew where this case was going. We couldn't stop her blood from clotting internally. My mind began to race. One of these days she was going to take out a vital organ. She must know this. Or did she? How had she endured the serial amputation of her limbs? Was she brave? In denial? Are they the same thing? And then there was the question of my interaction with her. Would a neutral stance convey hopelessness? Yet an upbeat, hopeful demeanor seemed inappropriate. To provide comfort—no argument with that goal—still required a manner that could be misconstrued. Shouldn't I wait to see what **her** attitude was, then adapt accordingly? Just don't be solemn, under any circumstance.*

In fact, she was gravely ill and was transferred to the ICU shortly after her arrival on our floor.

Worse than the hours was the work itself. Every test result, procedure, order, and incident was in some way processed through the intern. I wish I could say it was interesting work most of the time, but actually I felt more like busboy, waiter, and cook to an endlessly demanding room, for incredibly long shifts. The volume of tasks suffocated, and I was relentlessly needled by pages on the beeper, each delivering a new action item. In the desensitization, patients became their diseases.

Even death had its procedures.

I met her only once, for a few minutes, before her transfer to ICU. She was in a private room, lying with a sheet that covered the stumps of her limbs. Her face, fixed in a mask of silent anguish, was turned to the side and made no eye contact. She stared off into a middle distance, holding a pain no one could imagine or understand. Nothing was said.

In that moment I realized that my fear of the hospital had actually receded. I had replaced it with another emotion.

The moment broke a spell, the spell of my self-pity.
She was not "the DIC."
Her name was Nancy.

POSTSCRIPT

I never heard anything further about Nancy, as was the case for almost every other person who came through the medicine ward turbine. They all arrived at the height of illness and were focused on getting away as soon as possible, which I could certainly relate to.

Improbably, Mandy switched into psychiatry.

AFTERWORD

A DERMATOLOGIST, A NEUROSURGEON, and a psychiatrist walk into a bar. After a couple rounds of martinis they get into a pissing contest over who has the toughest job.

"*The way disease presents within the skin is notoriously variable,*" says the dermatologist. "*No two rashes mean the same thing.*"

"*If I so much as twitch, the results can be catastrophic,*" says the neurosurgeon. "*No two brains look the same.*"

"*The depth of human misery knows no bounds,*" says the psychiatrist. "*No two patients have the same experience.*"

Unable to move each other, the trio turn to the bartender to decide.

"*Well, how do you treat your patients?*" asks the bartender.

"*Mostly... I give them steroids,*" says the dermatologist.

"*Mostly... I study their scans before operating,*" says the neurosurgeon.

The psychiatrist hesitates. He stares down at his olive. After an interminable pause that all but signals defeat, he looks up at the bartender, forlorn. Then his face changes, and after another couple of beats, he concedes, with a wink,

"Mostly… I dance, one partner at a time."

ACKNOWLEDGMENTS

THIS PROJECT BEGAN AS AN IMPROMPTU vignette written on a cloudy day near Playa del Carmen. One thing led to the other and before long I found myself writing in every spare moment. Writing, like cooking, can be done by oneself, but is always enhanced by feedback from trusted epicureans. I am lucky to have friends, colleagues, and family far better read.

To Teresa Sullivan and Dr. Rob Goldstein, my deepest thanks for your honest critique and unwavering encouragement through the earliest drafts of these stories. Your support put a steady hand on the joystick I was rattling around.

It's safe to say everyone could do with a stalwart editor in life, and I was indeed fortunate to have crossed paths with Elizabeth Zack. Specialists writing for a general audience should always be concerned about whether the technical has been sufficiently explained. Thank you Elizabeth for your expertise in honing clarity within these cases, and for imparting your wisdom about how to tell a story.

To the crackerjack professionals at Luminare Press, Kim Harper-Kennedy, Claire Flint Last, and Patricia Marshall, thank you for doing what you do so well: shaping words and ideas into a book.

A special thanks to Drs. Roger Granet and Joseph Goldberg. In addition to invaluable editorial insights, you both gave me what every first-time author needs from established writers, but is so very hard to find—attention, kindness, and validation.

I want to thank the following individuals who generously gave their time to read manuscript drafts at various stages of development: Dr. Sandra Cohen, Frank Rubino, Jennie Dunham, Jack Tuchman, Vincent Mierlak, and Rachel Russell. Your enthusiasm helped keep the project, and my spirits, afloat.

Two colleagues must be acknowledged for planting the seed within me many years ago to write, and to trust my instincts: the late Samuel Perry, MD and the late Ethel Person, MD. They are missed by the many they touched.

I am indebted beyond words to my wife, Bronwyn O'Neil, and my children, Deryn and Donovan. Thank you for the many hats you three wore throughout this long project: editor, designer, sounding board, therapist, cheerleader. Most of all, thank you for your patience and support indulging my dream.

Finally, I want to thank all the patients I've worked with over the years—for entrusting your care, and in the process allowing me to have a most meaningful career.

Printed in Great Britain
by Amazon